Spelling and Vocabulary

Senior Author
Shane Templeton

Consultant
Rosa Maria Peña

HOUGHTON MIFFLIN

Boston • Atlanta • Dallas • Denver • Geneva, Illinois • Princeton, New Jersey • Palo Alto

Acknowledgments

For each of the selections listed below, grateful acknowledgment is made for permission to excerpt and/or reprint original or copyrighted material as follows:

Excerpt from *Clyde Monster,* by Robert L. Crowe. Text copyright ©1976 by Robert L. Crowe. Adapted and reprinted by permission of the publisher, E. P. Dutton, a division of Penguin Books USA Inc.

Illustrations by Patience Brewster from *Good as New,* by Barbara Douglass. Illustrations copyright ©1982 by Patience Brewster. Reprinted by permission of Lothrop, Lee & Shephard Books, a division of William Morrow & Company, Inc.

Illustrations from *Ira Sleeps Over,* by Bernard Waber. Copyright ©1972 by Bernard Waber. Reprinted by permission of Houghton Mifflin Company.

Excerpt and illustrations from "The Man and His Caps" in *Carousels* from *Houghton Mifflin Reading,* by Durr, et al. Copyright ©1986 by Houghton Mifflin Company. Reprinted by permission of Houghton Mifflin Company. All rights reserved.

Excerpt and illustrations from *We Are Best Friends,* by Aliki. Copyright ©1982 by Aliki Brandenberg. Reprinted by permission of Greenwillow Books, a division of William Morrow & Company, Inc. and The Bodley Head.

Illustrations from *Willaby*, by Rachel Isadora. Copyright ©1977 by Rachel Isadora. Reprinted with the permission of Simon & Schuster Books for Young Readers, an imprint of Simon & Schuster Children's Publishing Division.

Credits

Illustration   Mary Jane Begin **60** (b); Aliki Brandenberg **151**; Patience Brewster **135**; Maxie Chambliss **207, 209, 211, 213, 215, 217, 219, 221, 223**; Robert L. Crowe **167**; Jane Dyer **183**; Jennifer Harris **78**; Jamichael Henterly **88**; Rachel Isadora **120**; Tim Jones **101** (t), **133** (t), **166** (t), **178** (t); Juli Koontz **13–34, 37–38, 41–42, 47–48, 80** (b), **118** (t), **122** (b), **128** (b), **144** (b), **146** (b), **154** (b), **160** (b), **176** (b), **181** (t); Dora Leder **11–12, 60** (t), **61, 66–67, 69, 71** (t), **76** (b), **77, 81–82, 85–86, 87** (t), **101–103, 92–93, 98–99, 107–108, 113–114, 117, 118** (b), **119, 124–125, 130–131, 133–134, 139–140, 145–146, 149–150, 156–157, 161–162, 165–166, 172–173, 178** (b), **179, 181** (b), **182, 187–190**; Karen Schmidt **7–10, 55–59, 63–65, 70–71, 73–75, 79–80, 83, 87, 89–91, 95–97, 105–106, 109, 111–112, 115, 121–123, 127, 128** (t), **129, 136–138, 141, 143, 144** (t), **147, 152–153, 154** (t), **155, 159, 160** (t), **163, 167–171, 175, 176** (t), **177, 183–184, 185,** Kangaroo Pocket Card; Derek Steele **72**; Bernard Waber **104**

Assignment Photography   Cathy Copeland **12** (t, b); Allan Landau **110, 126**; Steve Nelson **62, 94, 100**; Tony Scarpetta **11, 12** (m); Dorey A. Sparre **148**

Photography   **13** (bananas), (Collie & Sheep dog), **15** (yellow bird), **17** (balloons), **19** (basket), **21** (key), (cats), **22** (robot), (rooster), **23** (flower), (butterfly) Image Copyright ©1997 PhotoDisc, Inc. **23** (bear) Johnny Johnson/Tony Stone Images **25** (farm) Gay Baumgarner/Tony Stone Images **26** (baseball) Image Copyright ©1997 PhotoDisc, Inc. **26** (garden) Ryan-Beyer/Tony Stone Images **26** (horn), **27** (bananas) Image Copyright ©1997 PhotoDisc, Inc. **30** (volcano) © Ken Sakamoto/Black Star/PNI **31** (beetle), (lettuce), (basket) Image Copyright ©1997 PhotoDisc, Inc. **41** (web) © Archive Photos, 1994/PNI **44** (elephant) © Wood River Gallery, 1995/PNI **45** (robot), (key), (bananas), **46** (carrots), **47** (basket), **48** (Collie dog) Image Copyright ©1997 PhotoDisc, Inc. **48** (bear) Johnny Johnson/Tony Stone Images **48** (web), **51** (web) © Archive Photos, 1994/PNI **50** (farm) Gay Baumgarner/Tony Stone Images **53** (mat), **61** (rabbits) Image Copyright ©1997 PhotoDisc, Inc.

2000 Impression
Copyright ©1998 by Houghton Mifflin Company. All rights reserved.

Printed in U.S.A.

ISBN: 0-395-85528-4

56789-B-04 03 02 01 00 99

Contents

Cycle One

Unit 1

Spelling the Short a Sound   57

- Vocabulary
- Writing
- Proofreading
- Special Words for Writing: *the, and, a*
- Phonics and Spelling
  Rhyming Words

Unit 2

Spelling the Short i Sound   63

- Vocabulary
- Writing
- Proofreading
- Special Words for Writing: *to, of, is*
- Phonics and Spelling
  Rhyming Words

Unit 3

Review   69

- Dictionary
  ABC Order
- Literature and Writing
  Literature
  Doghouse for Sale, by Donna Lugg Pape
  The Writing Process
  My Room

Contents

TABLE OF CONTENTS

4

Contents

TABLE OF CONTENTS

Contents

TABLE OF CONTENTS

6

Contents

TABLE OF CONTENTS

7

Picture Clues

Consonant Sounds and Letters

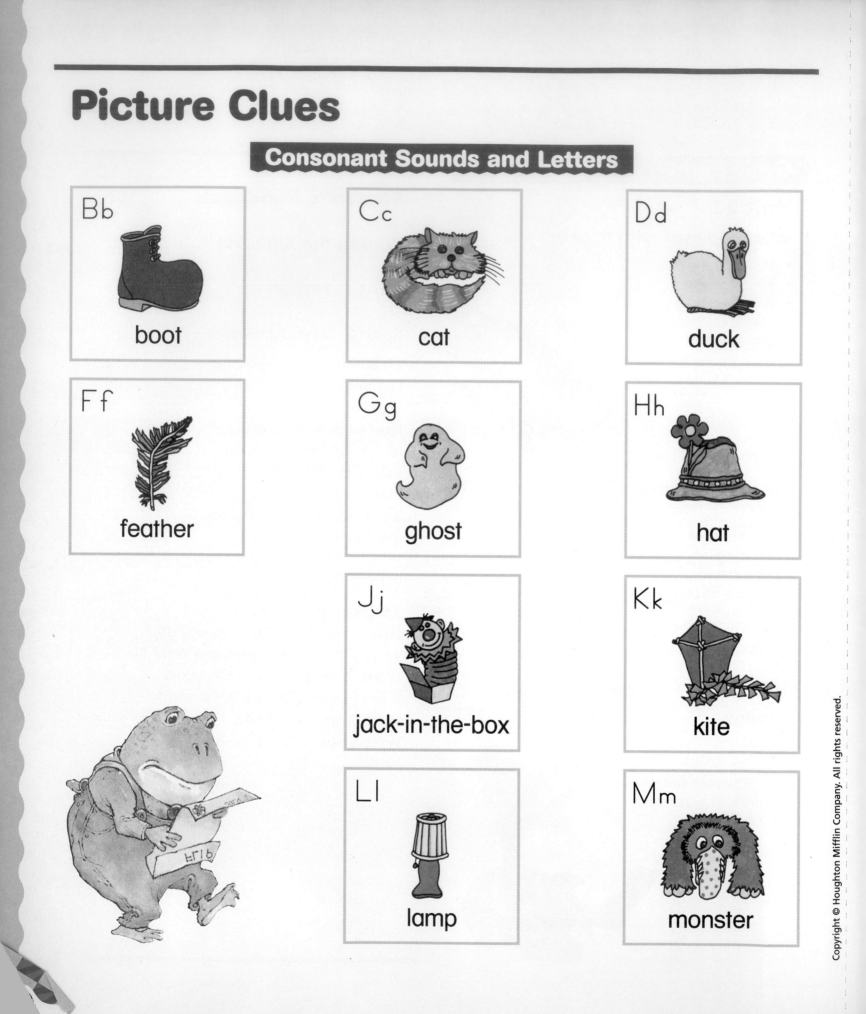

Bb — boot

Cc — cat

Dd — duck

Ff — feather

Gg — ghost

Hh — hat

Jj — jack-in-the-box

Kk — kite

Ll — lamp

Mm — monster

Consonant Sounds and Letters

N n — nest

P p — pig

Q q — quarter

R r — rabbit

S s — sock

T t — tiger

V v — vest

W w — worm

Y y — yo-yo

Z z — zipper

Picture Clues (continued)

Vowel Sounds and Letters

Aa
apple
apron

Ee
egg
eel

Ii
igloo
ice

Oo
octopus
ocean

Uu
umbrella

Phonics: Sounds and Letters

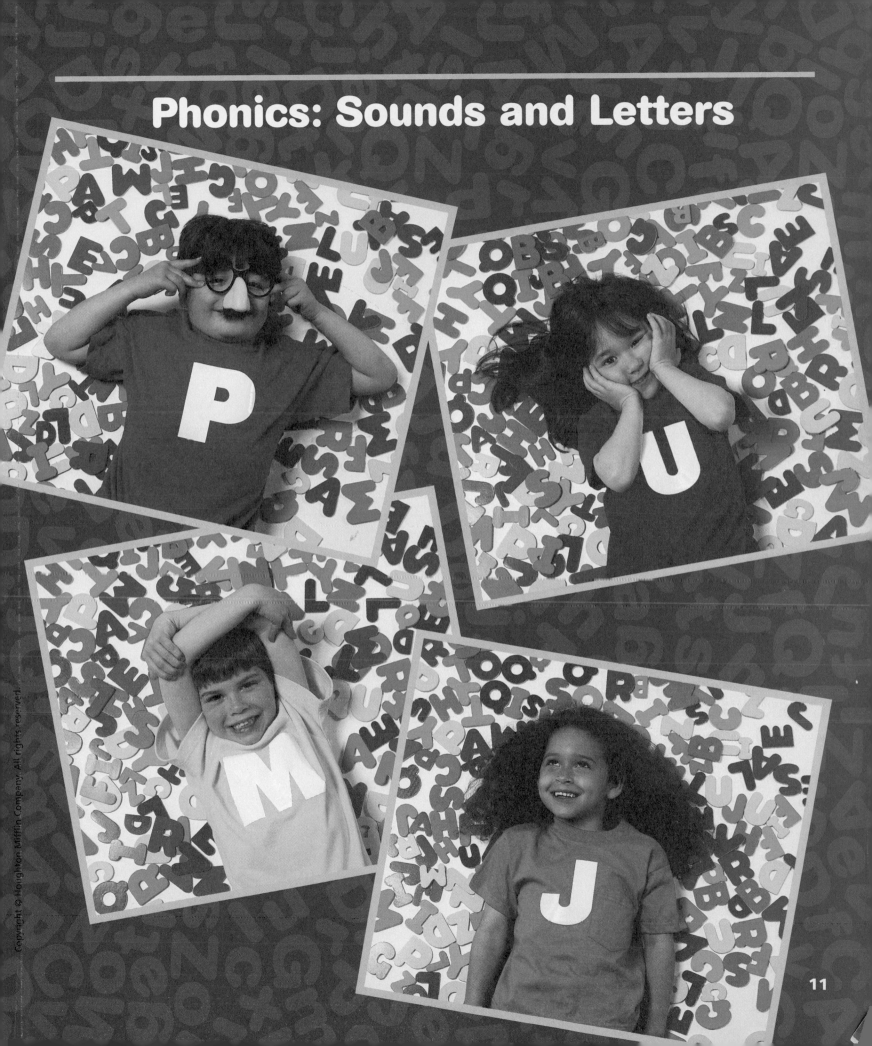

Name _____

1 Following Directions

Circle each picture that is red.

Color each picture of a toy.

Mark an **X** on each picture of food.

Draw a line under each picture of a dog.

PHONICS

Copyright © Houghton Mifflin Company. All rights reserved.

Skill: Children will practice skills needed to follow printed directions in subsequent lessons and units.

Home Activity: Give your child additional practice in following directions by asking him or her to circle, draw a line under, or mark an X on pictures you identify in a newspaper or a magazine.

13

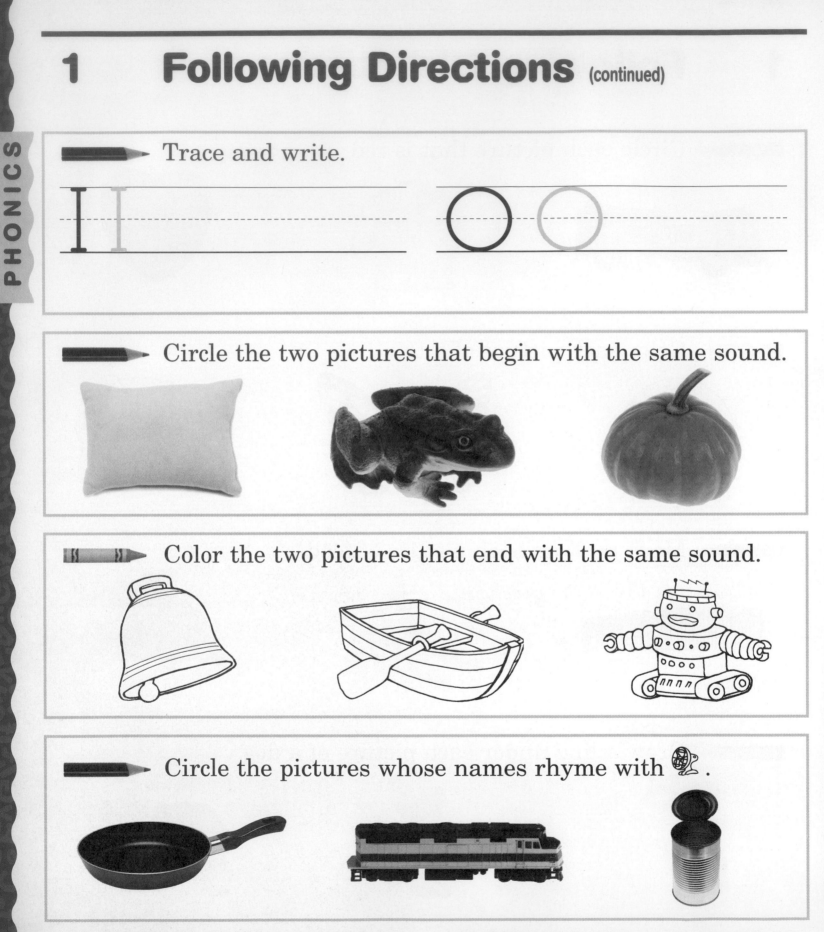

1 Following Directions (continued)

Trace and write.

Circle the two pictures that begin with the same sound.

Color the two pictures that end with the same sound.

Circle the pictures whose names rhyme with 🐟.

Skill: Children will practice skills needed to follow printed directions in subsequent lessons and units.

Home Activity: Have your child draw pictures of pairs of items whose names begin with the same sound. *Example:* **d**og, **d**ish

Name _____

2 Listening and Writing: Ss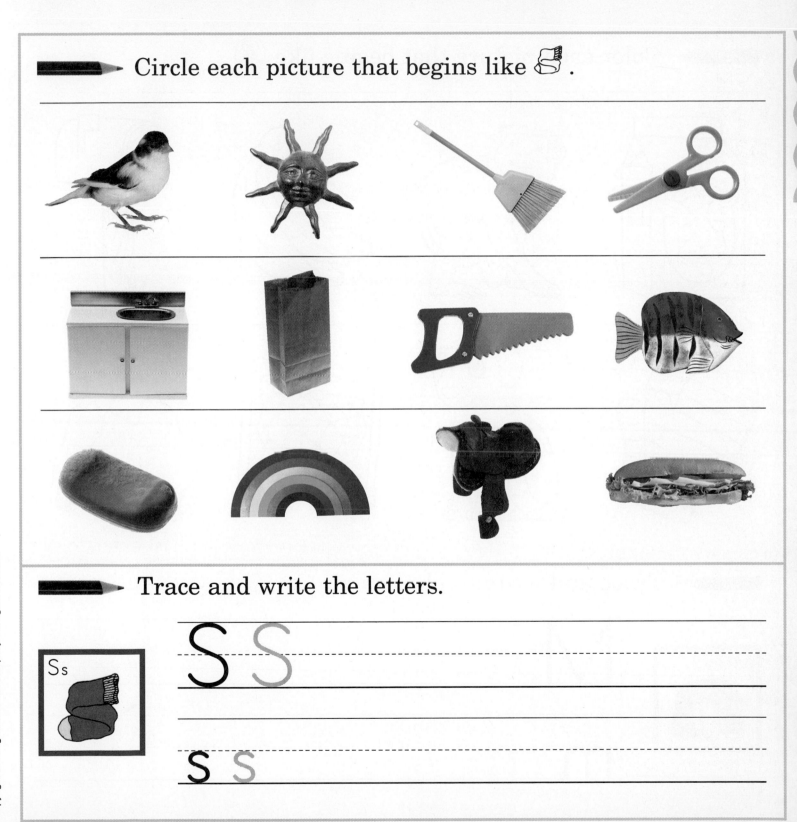

Circle each picture that begins like 🧦.

Trace and write the letters.

S S

s s

Skill: Children will circle pictures whose names begin with the |s| sound. They will associate this sound with the letter **s** and will write upper- and lowercase forms. **Picture clue: sock**

Home Activity: Have your child trace the upper- and lowercase forms of **s** with a finger. Ask your child to illustrate one of these words that begin with the letter **s**: **soup, suitcase, submarine.**

PHONICS

3 Listening and Writing: Mm

Color each picture that begins like 🐵.

Trace and write the letters.

Mm

M M

m m

Skill: Children will color pictures whose names begin with the |m| sound. They will associate this sound with the letter **m** and will write upper- and lowercase forms. **Picture clue: monster**

Home Activity: Have your child name the pictures on this page that begin like **monster**. Together, find in a book or a magazine pictures whose names begin with the letter **m**.

4   Listening and Writing: T t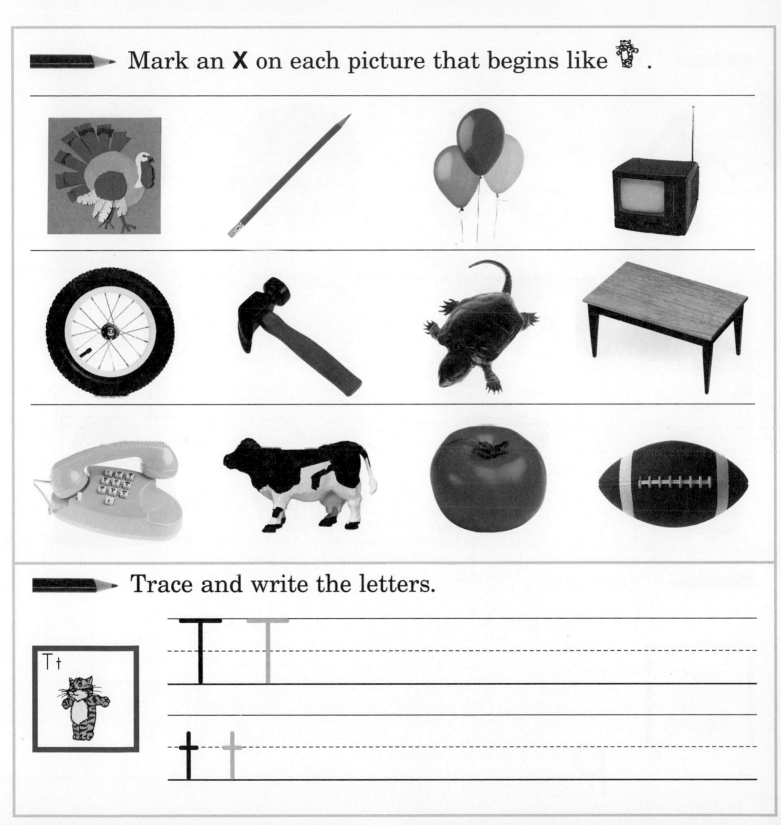

Mark an **X** on each picture that begins like 🐯 .

Trace and write the letters.

T t

PHONICS

Skill: Children will mark pictures whose names begin with the |t| sound. They will associate this sound with the letter **t** and will write upper- and lowercase forms. **Picture clue: tiger**

Home Activity: Have your child trace the upper- and lowercase forms of **t** with a finger. Together, think of people's names that begin with the letter **t**.

5 Listening and Writing: Pp

✏️ Draw a line under each picture that begins like 🐷 .

✏️ Trace and write the letters.

P P

p p

Skill: Children will underline pictures whose names begin with the |p| sound. They will associate this sound with the letter **p** and will write upper- and lowercase forms. **Picture clue: pig**

Home Activity: Have your child name the pictures on this page that begin like **pig**. Together, make up tongue twisters, using words that begin with the letter **p**. *Example: Paul pats porcupines.*

6   Listening and Writing: N n

Circle each picture that begins like .

Trace and write the letters.

N N

n n

Skill: Children will circle pictures whose names begin with the |n| sound. They will associate this sound with the letter **n** and will write upper- and lowercase forms. **Picture clue: nest**

Home Activity: Have your child trace the upper- and lowercase forms of **n** with a finger. Ask your child to cut out from magazines or catalogs pictures whose names begin with the letter **n**.

7 Listening and Writing: Cc

Color each picture that begins like 🐱.

Trace and write the letters.

Cc

C C

c c

Skill: Children will color pictures whose names begin with the |k| sound. They will associate this sound with the letter **c** and will write upper- and lowercase forms. **Picture clue: cat**

Home Activity: Have your child name the pictures on this page that begin like **cat**. Ask your child to illustrate one of these words that begin with the letter **c: camera, caboose, cave.**

Name _____

8 Listening and Writing: Kk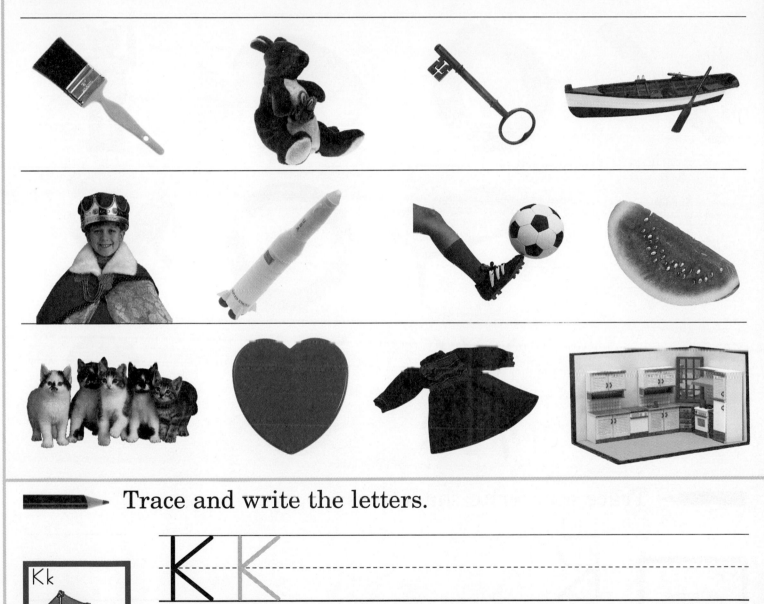

Mark an **X** on each picture that begins like 🪁 .

Trace and write the letters.

Kk

K K

k k

Skill: Children will mark pictures whose names begin with the |k| sound. They will associate this sound with the letter **k** and will write upper- and lowercase forms. **Picture clue: kite**

Home Activity: Have your child trace the upper- and lowercase forms of **k** with a finger. Ask your child to illustrate one of these words that begin with the letter **k: kettle, keyboard, koala.**

Draw a line under each picture that begins like 🐰.

Trace and write the letters.

Rr

R R

r r

Skill: Children will underline pictures whose names begin with the |r| sound. They will associate this sound with the letter **r** and will write upper- and lowercase forms. **Picture clue: rabbit**

Home Activity: Have your child name the pictures on this page that begin like **rabbit**. Ask your child to point out and name items in your home whose names begin with the letter **r**.

Name _____

10 Listening and Writing: Bb 👢

✏️ Circle each picture that begins like 👢.

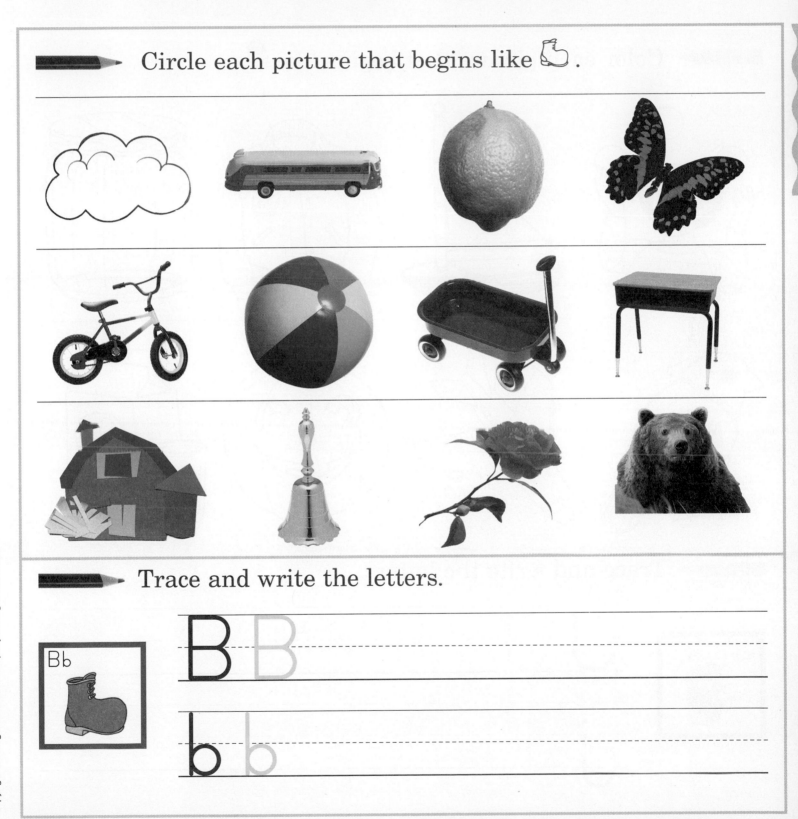

✏️ Trace and write the letters.

Bb 👢

B B

b b

Skill: Children will circle pictures whose names begin with the |b| sound. They will associate this sound with the letter **b** and will write upper- and lowercase forms. **Picture clue: boot**

Home Activity: Have your child trace the upper- and lowercase forms of **b** with a finger. Together, think of people's names that begin with the letter **b**.

23

Color each picture that begins like 🪅.

Trace and write the letters.

J J

j j

Skill: Children will color pictures whose names begin with the |j| sound. They will associate this sound with the letter **j** and will write upper- and lowercase forms. **Picture clue: jack-in-the-box**

Home Activity: Have your child name the pictures on this page that begin like **jack-in-the-box**. Ask your child to illustrate one of these words that begin with the letter **j**: **jewels, jungle**.

12 Listening and Writing: F f

Mark an **X** on each picture that begins like 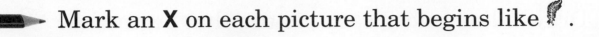 .

Trace and write the letters.

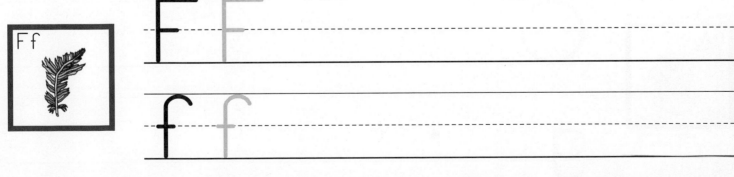

Skill: Children will mark pictures whose names begin with the |f| sound. They will associate this sound with the letter **f** and will write upper- and lowercase forms. **Picture clue: feather**

Home Activity: Have your child trace the upper- and lowercase forms of **f** with a finger. Ask your child to name several numbers that begin with the letter **f**.

Listening and Writing: G g

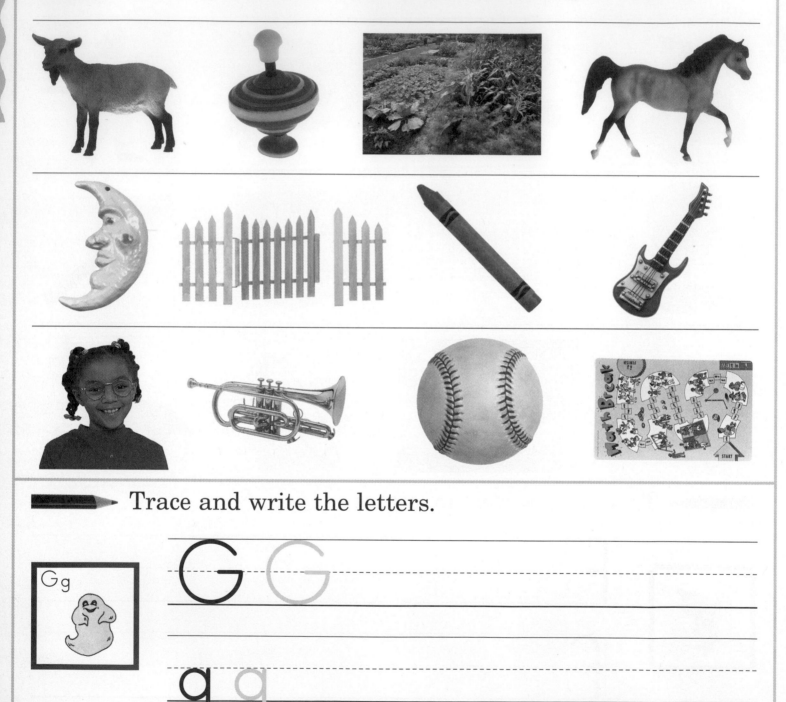

Draw a line under each picture that begins like 👻.

Trace and write the letters.

Gg

G G

g g

Skill: Children will underline pictures whose names begin with the |g| sound. They will associate this sound with the letter **g** and will write upper- and lowercase forms. **Picture clue: ghost**

Home Activity: Have your child name the pictures on this page that begin like **ghost**. Together, find in a book or a magazine pictures whose names begin with the letter **g**.

14 Listening and Writing: Hh

Circle each picture that begins like 🎩 .

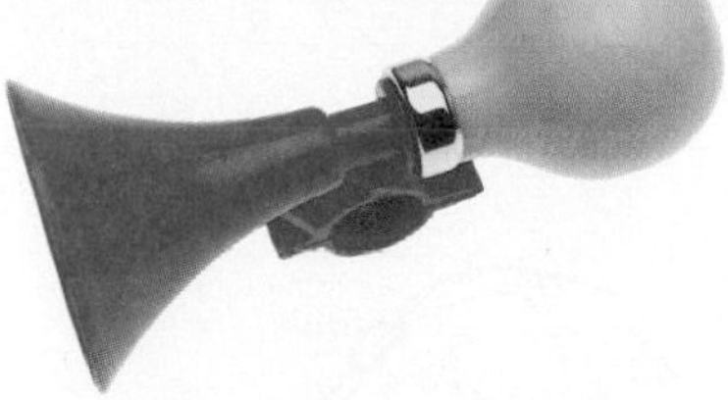

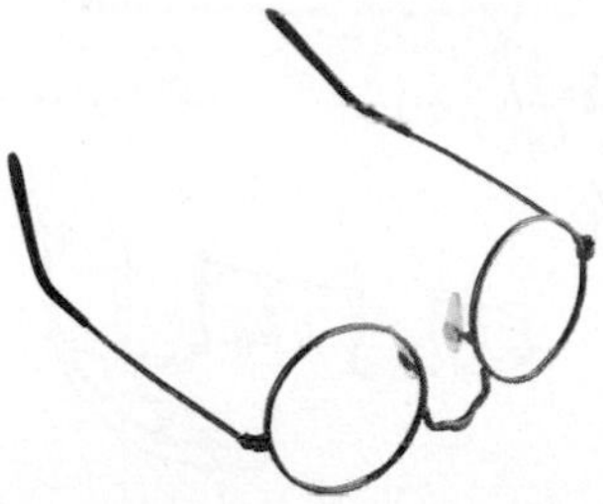

Trace and write the letters.

Hh

H H

h h

Skill: Children will circle pictures whose names begin with the |h| sound. They will associate this sound with the letter **h** and will write upper- and lowercase forms. **Picture clue: hat**

Home Activity: Have your child trace the upper- and lowercase forms of h with a finger. Together, think of animals whose names begin with the letter h.

PHONICS

Color each picture that begins like 🦆.

Trace and write the letters.

Dd

D D

d d

Skill: Children will color pictures whose names begin with the |d| sound. They will associate this sound with the letter **d** and will write upper- and lowercase forms. **Picture clue: duck**

Home Activity: Have your child name the pictures on this page that begin like **duck**. Ask your child to cut out from magazines or catalogs pictures whose names begin with the letter **d**.

Name _____

16   Listening and Writing: W w

Mark an **X** on each picture that begins like 🐛.

Trace and write the letters.

Skill: Children will mark pictures whose names begin with the |w| sound. They will associate this sound with the letter **w** and will write upper- and lowercase forms. **Picture clue: worm**

Home Activity: Have your child trace the upper- and lowercase forms of **w** with a finger. Together, make up tongue twisters, using words that begin with the letter **w**. *Example: Will Willy wait?*

29

✏️ Draw a line under each picture that begins like 🎽.

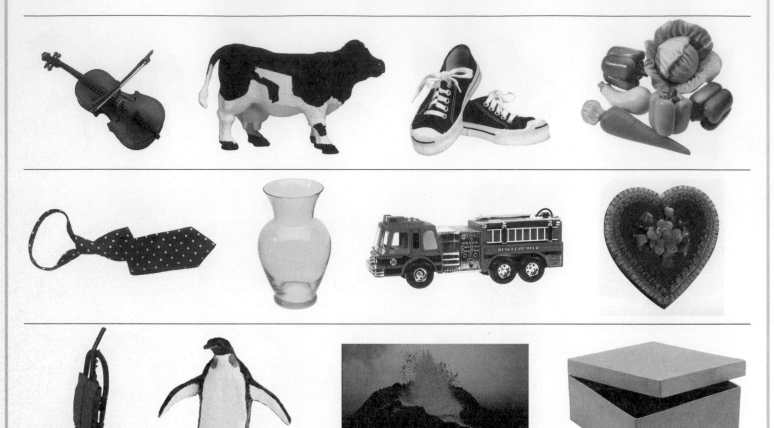

✏️ Trace and write the letters.

V v 🎽

V ∨

V ∨

Skill: Children will underline pictures whose names begin with the |v| sound. They will associate this sound with the letter **v** and will write upper- and lowercase forms. **Picture clue: vest**

Home Activity: Have your child name the pictures on this page that begin like **vest**. Ask your child to illustrate one of these words that begin with the letter **v: village, van**.

18 Listening and Writing: L l 🪔

PHONICS

> Circle each picture that begins like 🪔 .

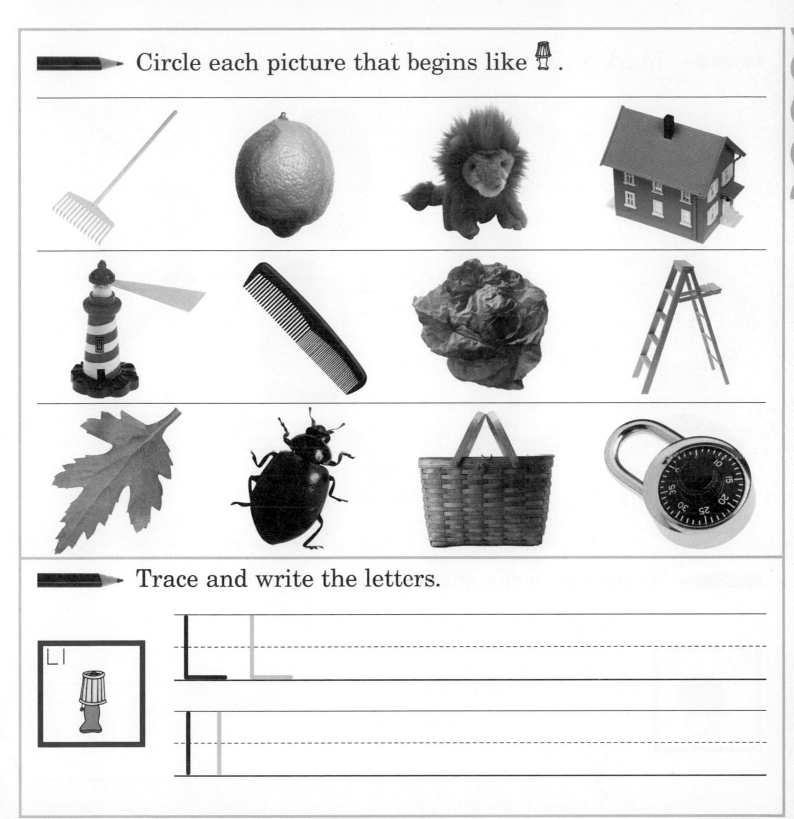

> Trace and write the letters.

L l
🪔

Skill: Children will circle pictures whose names begin with the |l| sound. They will associate this sound with the letter **l** and will write upper- and lowercase forms. **Picture clue: lamp**

Home Activity: Have your child trace the upper- and lowercase forms of **l** with a finger. Together, think of people's names that begin with the letter **l**.

19   Listening and Writing: Yy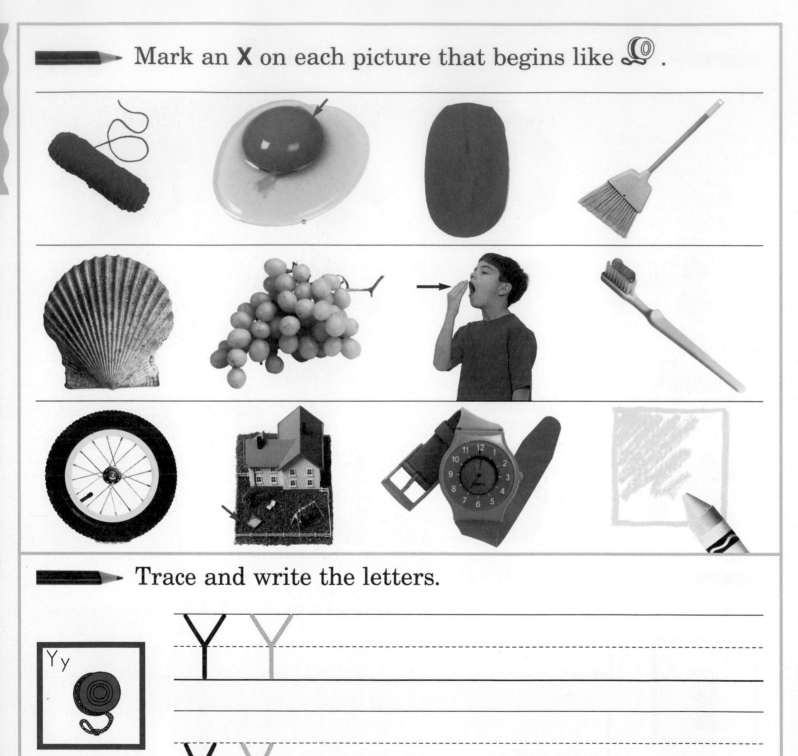

Mark an **X** on each picture that begins like 🪀 .

Trace and write the letters.

Yy

Y Y

y y

32

Copyright © Houghton Mifflin Company. All rights reserved.

Skill: Children will mark pictures whose names begin with the |y| sound. They will associate this sound with the letter **y** and will write upper- and lowercase forms. **Picture clue: yo-yo**

Home Activity: Have your child name the pictures on this page that begin like **yo-yo**. Ask your child to circle in a newspaper or a magazine words that begin with the letter **y**.

Name _____

20 Listening and Writing: Zz Z

PHONICS

Color each picture that begins like Z.

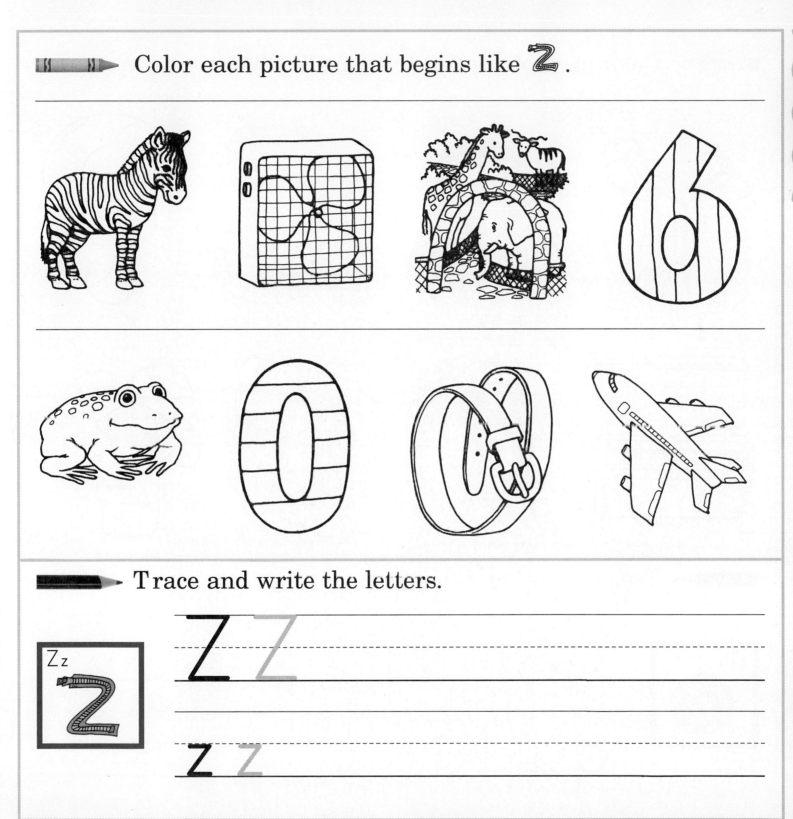

Trace and write the letters.

Zz Z

Zz

z z

Skill: Children will color pictures whose names begin with the |z| sound. They will associate this sound with the letter z and will write upper- and lowercase forms. **Picture clue: zipper**

Home Activity: Have your child trace the upper- and lowercase forms of z with a finger. Say some words aloud. Ask your child to clap after each word that begins with the letter z.

33

Color each picture that begins like .

Trace and write the letters.

Qu Qu

qu qu

Skill: Children will color pictures whose names begin with the |kw| sound. They will associate this sound with the letters **qu** and will write upper- and lowercase forms. **Picture clue: quarter**

Home Activity: Have your child name the pictures on this page that begin like **quarter**. Together, think of other words that begin with the letters **qu**. *Examples: quiet, quack, quit*

Name _____

✏️ Circle each picture with the 🍎 sound.

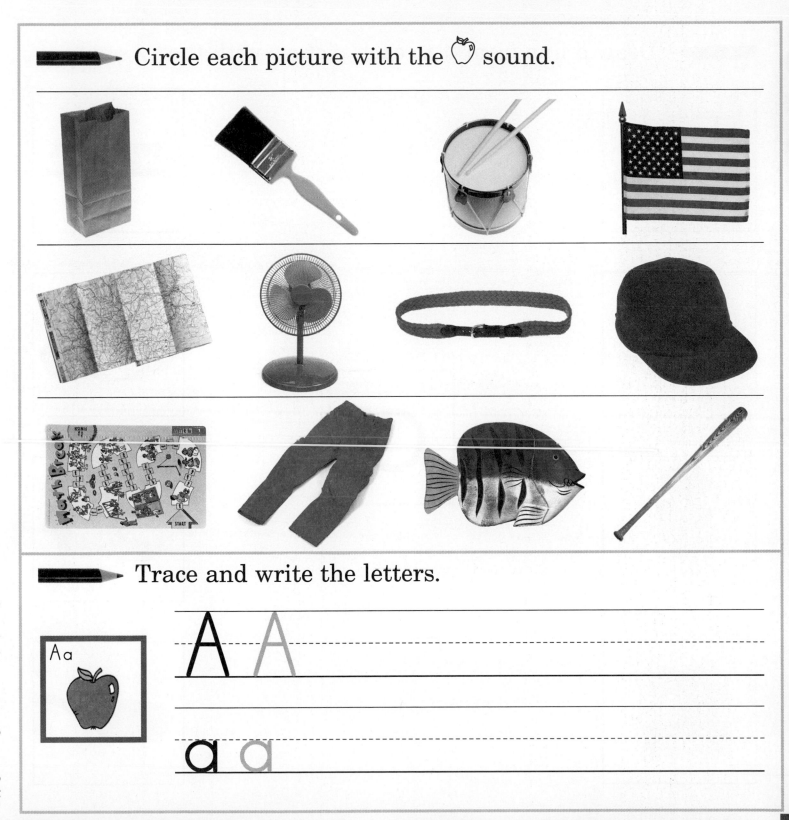

✏️ Trace and write the letters.

Aa 🍎

A A

a a

Skill: Children will circle pictures whose names begin with the |ă| sound. They will associate this sound with the letter **a** and will write upper- and lowercase forms. **Picture clue: apple**

Home Activity: Have your child trace the upper- and lowercase forms of **a** with a finger. Together, find in a book or a magazine pictures whose names have the **apple** sound.

22 Listening and Writing: Aa 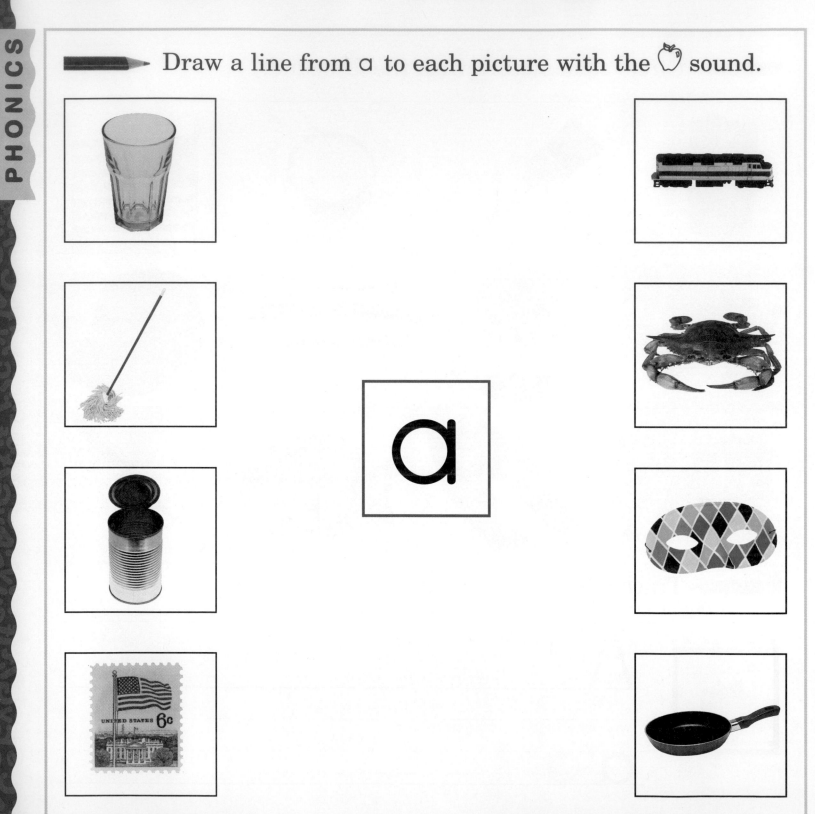 (continued)

Draw a line from a to each picture with the apple sound.

Skill: Children will match the letter **a** with pictures whose names have the |ă| sound. **Picture clue: apple**

Home Activity: Have your child name the pictures on this page that have the **apple** sound. Ask your child to point out and name items in your home whose names have the **apple** sound.

23 Listening and Writing: Ii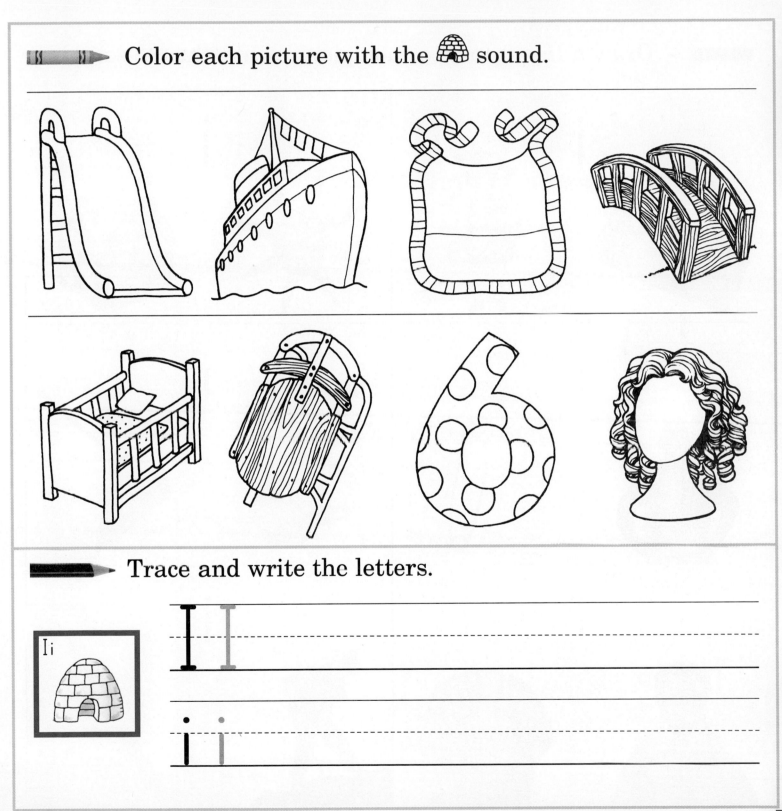

Color each picture with the 🏠 sound.

Trace and write the letters.

Ii

Skill: Children will color pictures whose names have the |ĭ| sound. They will associate this sound with the letter **i** and will write upper- and lowercase forms. **Picture clue: igloo**

Home Activity: Have your child trace the upper- and lowercase forms of **i** with a finger. Together, make a shopping list of things whose names have the **igloo** sound. *Examples: fish, milk, pins*

PHONICS

Draw a line from **i** to each picture with the 🏠 sound.

i   i

i   i

i   i

Skill: Children will match the letter **i** with pictures whose names have the |ĭ| sound. **Picture clue: igloo**

Home Activity: Have your child name the pictures on this page that have the **igloo** sound. Together, think of people's names that have the **igloo** sound.

24 Listening and Writing: ○○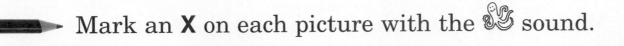

Mark an **X** on each picture with the 🐙 sound.

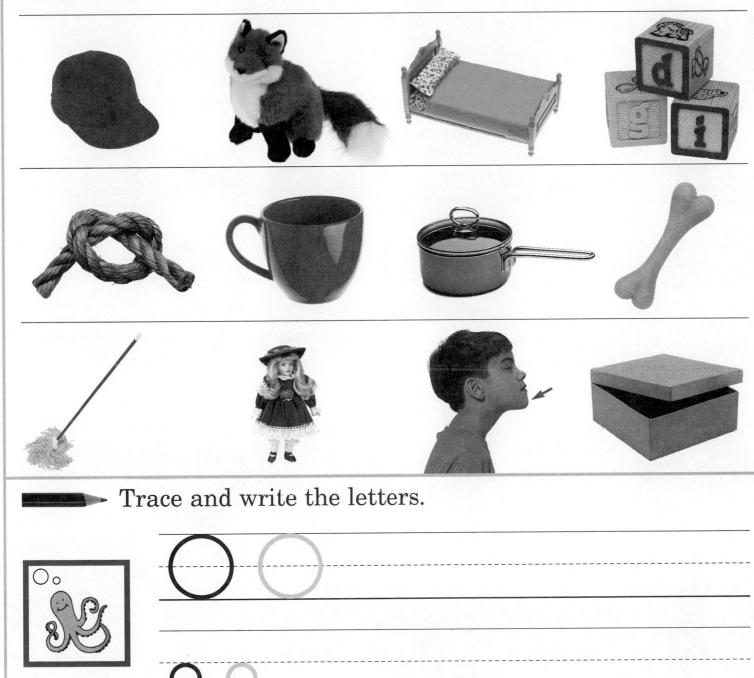

Trace and write the letters.

Skill: Children will mark pictures whose names have the |ŏ| sound. They will associate this sound with the letter **o** and will write upper- and lowercase forms. **Picture clue: octopus**

Home Activity: Have your child trace the upper- and lowercase forms of **o** with a finger. Ask your child to illustrate one of these words that have the **octopus** sound: **doll, shop.**

PHONICS

Write **o** next to each picture with the 🐙 sound.

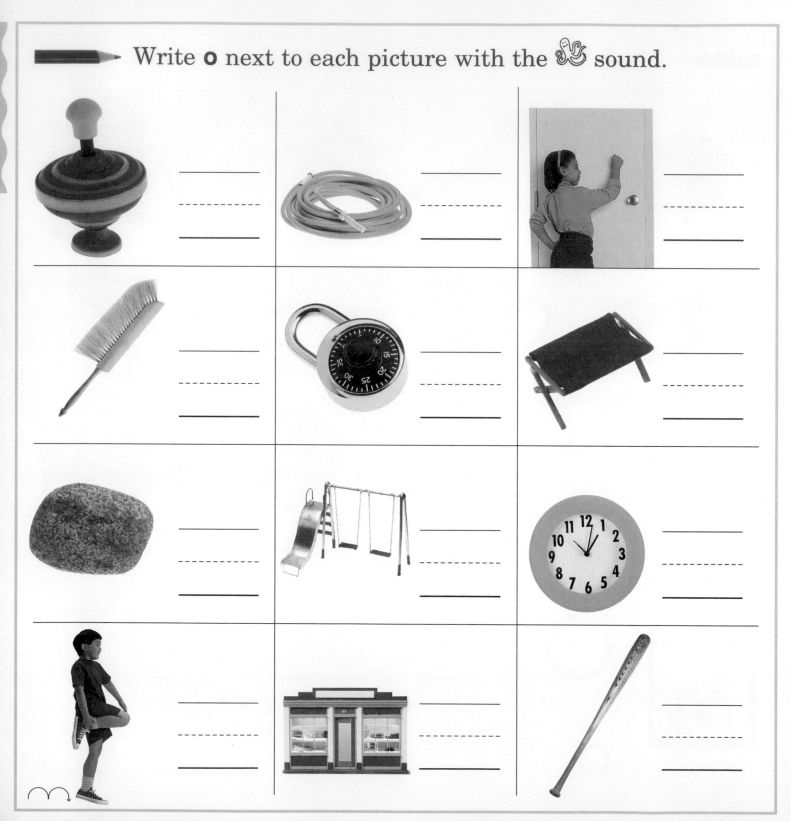

Skill: Children will write the letter **o** beside pictures whose names have the |ŏ| sound. **Picture clue: octopus**

Home Activity: Have your child name the pictures on this page that have the **octopus** sound. Ask your child to cut out from magazines pictures whose names have the **octopus** sound.

Name _____

25 Listening and Writing: E e ⬭

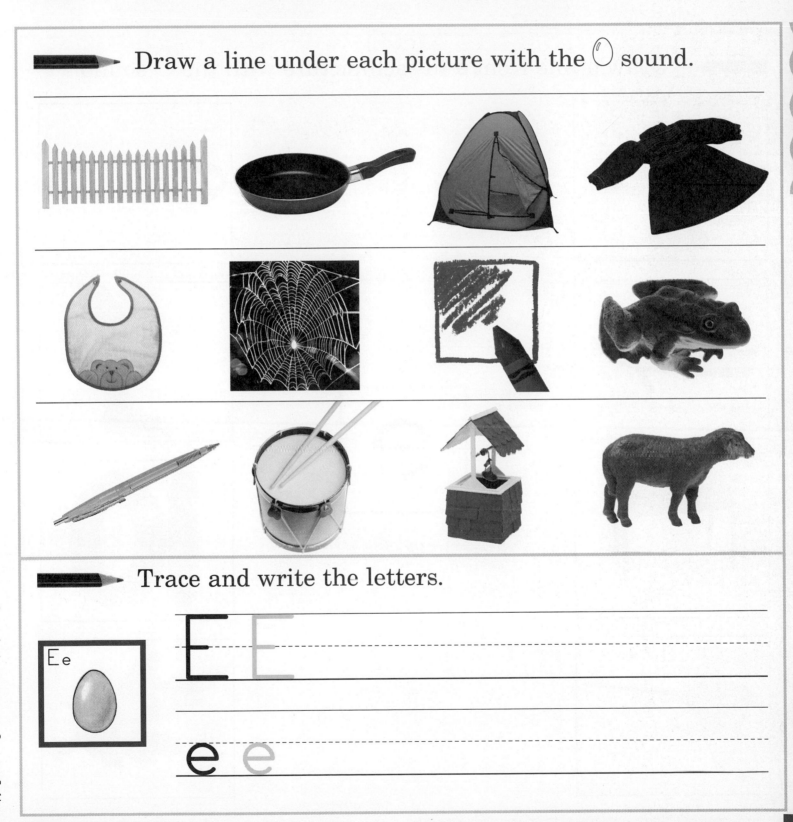

✏️➤ Draw a line under each picture with the ⬭ sound.

✏️➤ Trace and write the letters.

E e

E E

e e

PHONICS

Skill: Children will underline pictures whose names have the |ĕ| sound. They will associate this sound with the letter **e** and will write upper- and lowercase forms. **Picture clue:** egg

Home Activity: Have your child trace the upper- and lowercase forms of **e** with a finger. Together, think of some classroom items whose names have the **egg** sound. *Examples: desk, pen, bell*

41

25 Listening and Writing: E e ◌ (continued)

Draw a line from **e** to each picture with the ◌ sound.

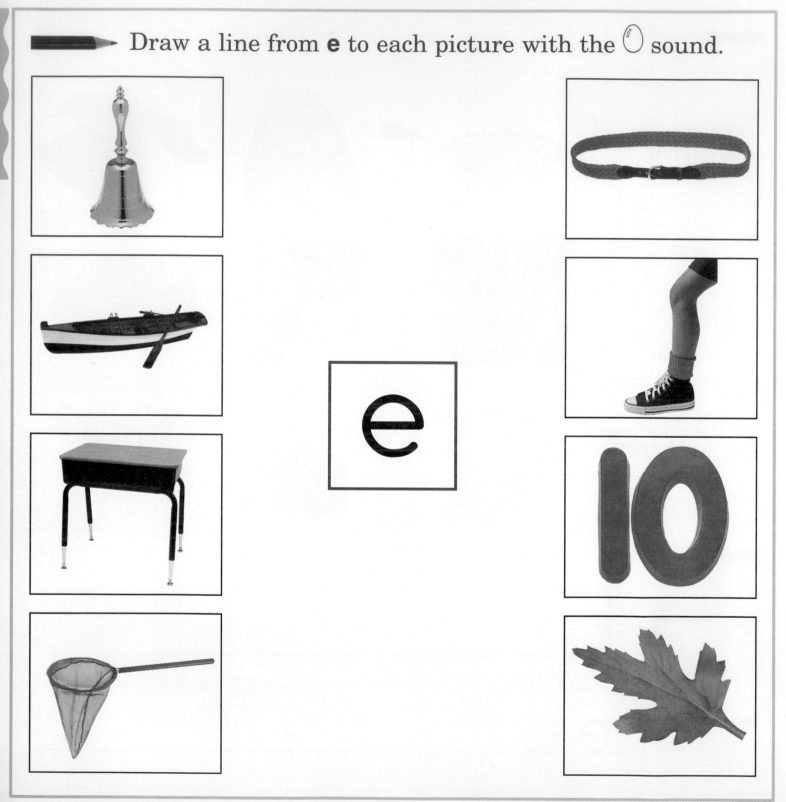

e

Skill: Children will match the letter **e** with pictures whose names have the |ĕ| sound. **Picture clue: egg**

Home Activity: Have your child name the pictures on this page that have the **egg** sound. Ask your child to illustrate one of these words that have the **egg** sound: **hen, sled, bench.**

26 Listening and Writing: Uu ☂

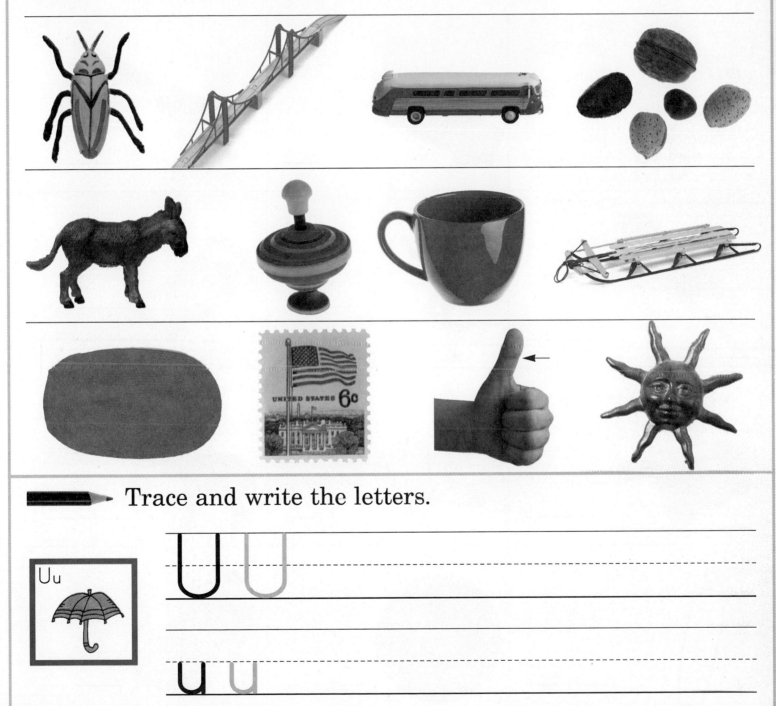

✏️ Circle each picture with the ☂ sound.

✏️ Trace and write the letters.

Uu ☂	U U
	u u

Skill: Children will circle pictures whose names have the |ŭ| sound. They will associate this sound with the letter **u** and will write upper- and lowercase forms. **Picture clue: umbrella**

Home Activity: Have your child trace the upper- and lowercase forms of **u** with a finger. Say the name for each picture above. Ask your child to clap after each word with the **umbrella** sound.

26 Listening and Writing: Uu 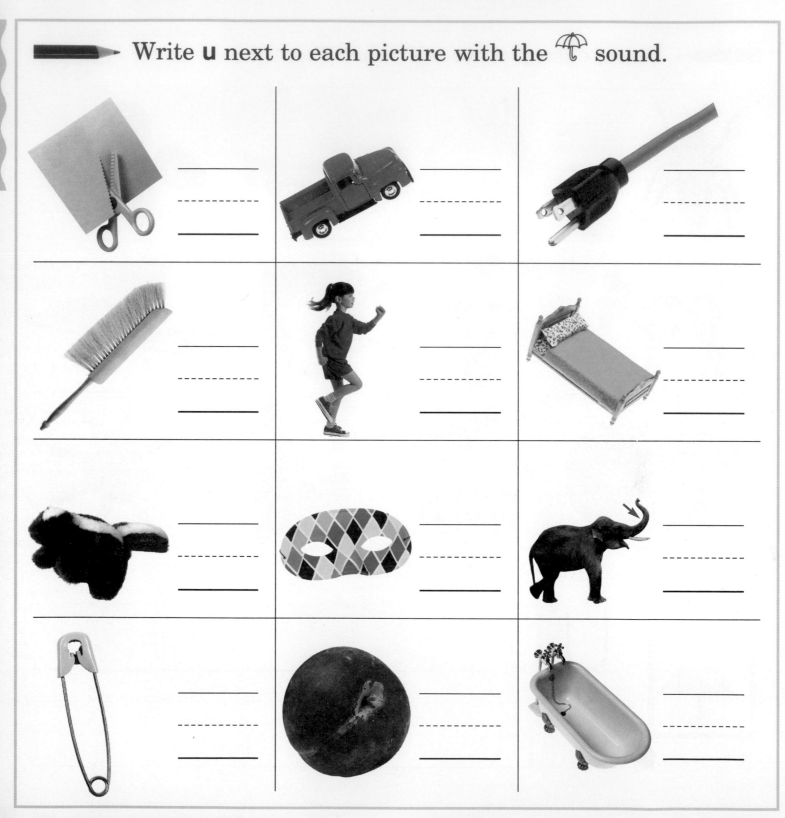 (continued)

Write **u** next to each picture with the ☂ sound.

Skill: Children will write the letter **u** beside pictures whose names have the |ŭ| sound. **Picture clue:** umbrella

Home Activity: Have your child name the pictures on this page that have the **umbrella** sound. Together, think of action words that have the **umbrella** sound. *Examples: run, jump, cut, hug*

27 Listening and Writing: Initial Consonants

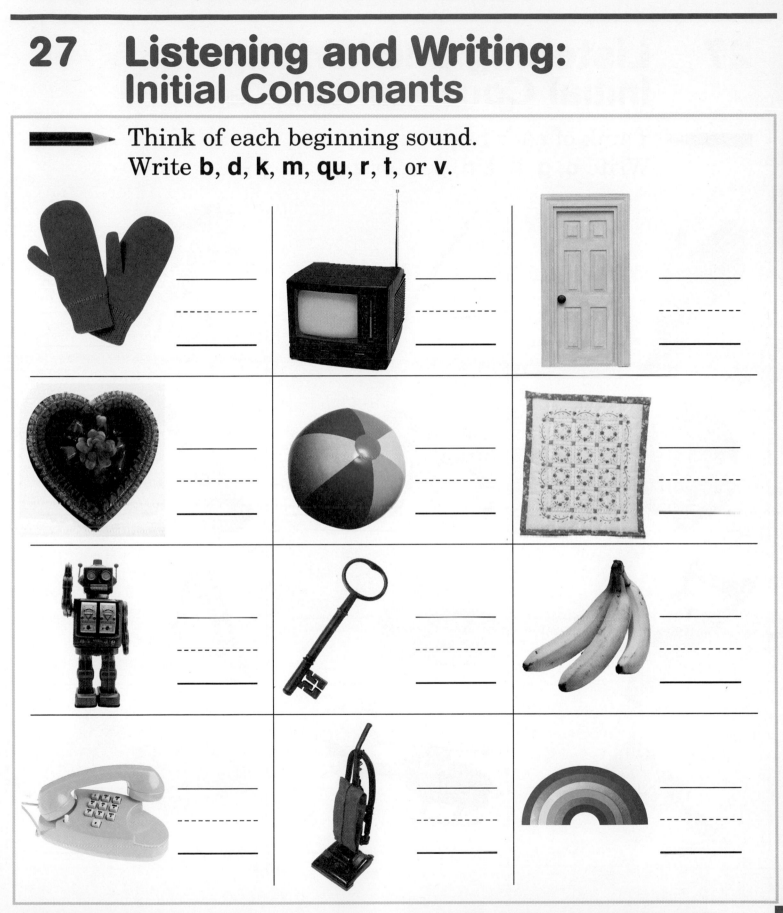

Think of each beginning sound.
Write **b**, **d**, **k**, **m**, **qu**, **r**, **t**, or **v**.

Skill: Children will write the letters that represent initial consonant sounds in picture names.

Home Activity: Say other simple words that begin with the consonant letters shown on this page. After each word, ask your child to name the letter or letters that spell the beginning sound.

27 Listening and Writing: Initial Consonants (continued)

Think of each beginning sound.
Write **c**, **g**, **h**, **l**, **n**, **p**, **s**, or **z**.

Skill: Children will write the letters that represent initial consonant sounds in picture names.

Home Activity: Together, list other words that begin with the consonant letters shown on this page. Ask your child to choose, copy, and illustrate one of the words on the list.

28 Listening and Writing: Final Consonants

Think of each ending sound. Write **k**, **m**, **n**, **p**, **s**, or **t**.

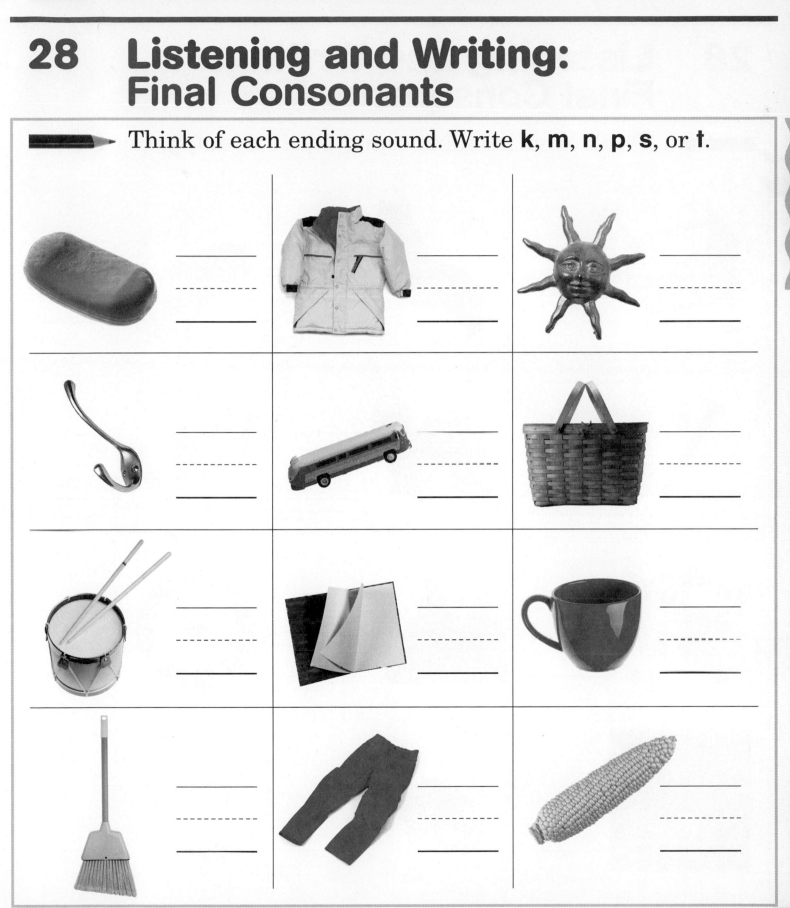

Skill: Children will write the letters that represent final consonant sounds in picture names.

Home Activity: Say the words **dress, farm, shirt, soup, fun,** and **cook**. After each word, ask your child to name the letter that spells the ending sound.

28 Listening and Writing: Final Consonants (continued)

Think of each ending sound. Write **b**, **d**, **f**, **g**, **l**, or **r**.

Skill: Children will write the letters that represent final consonant sounds in picture names.

Home Activity: Say the words **ear, bib, chief, big, red,** and **bowl**. After each word, ask your child to name the letter that spells the ending sound.

29 Listening and Writing: Consonants in Words

Think of each beginning sound.
Write **f**, **h**, **j**, **l**, **p**, **r**, **w**, or **y** to spell each word.

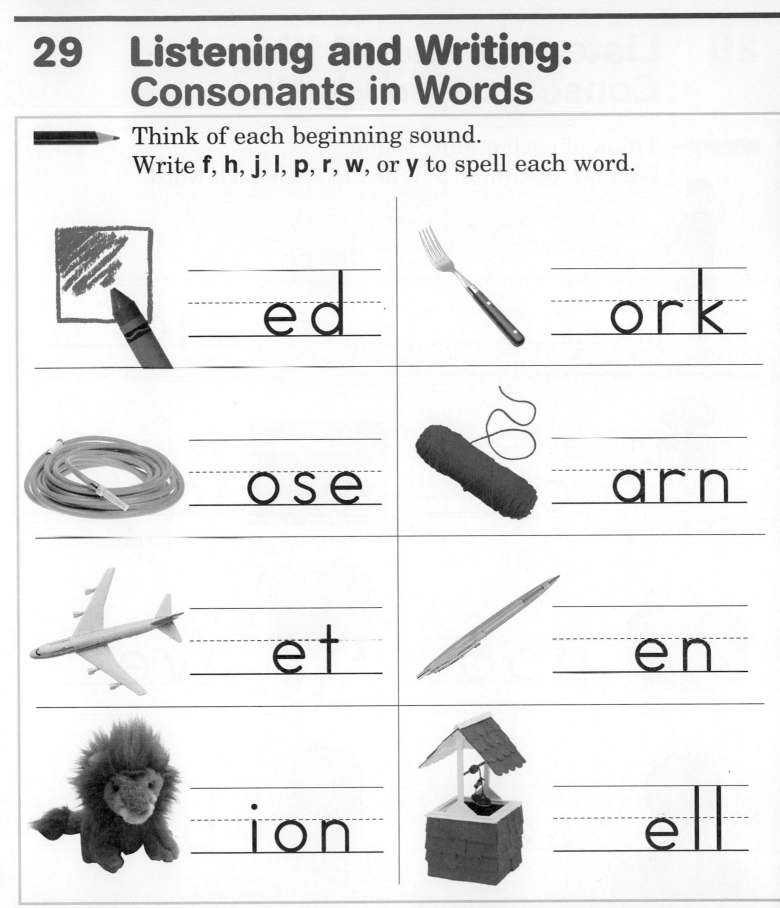

_ed

_ork

_ose

_arn

_et

_en

_ion

_ell

Skill: Children will write initial consonants to complete words.

Home Activity: Say sentences in which every word begins with one consonant letter shown on this page. *Example: Hot hens hate hats.* Have your child name the letter that begins each word.

Think of each ending sound.
Write **d**, **g**, **l**, **m**, **n**, **p**, **r**, or **t** to spell each word.

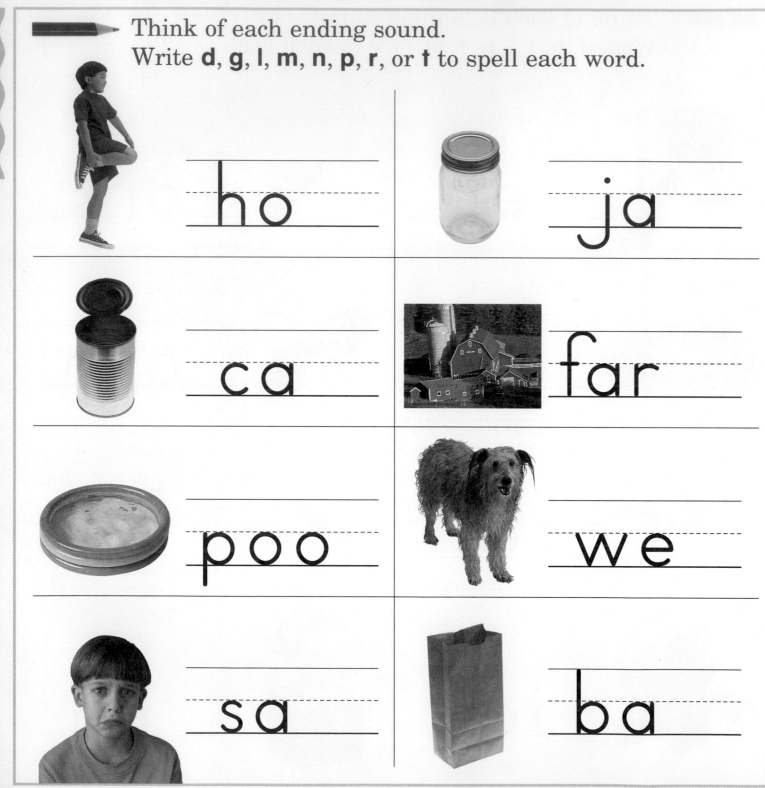

ho

ja

ca

far

poo

we

sa

ba

Skill: Children will write final consonants to complete words.

Home Activity: Say other words that end with the consonant letters shown on this page. After each word, ask your child to name the letter that spells the ending sound.

Name _____

30 Listening and Writing: Short Vowels

Think of each middle sound. Write **a**, **e**, **i**, **o**, or **u**.

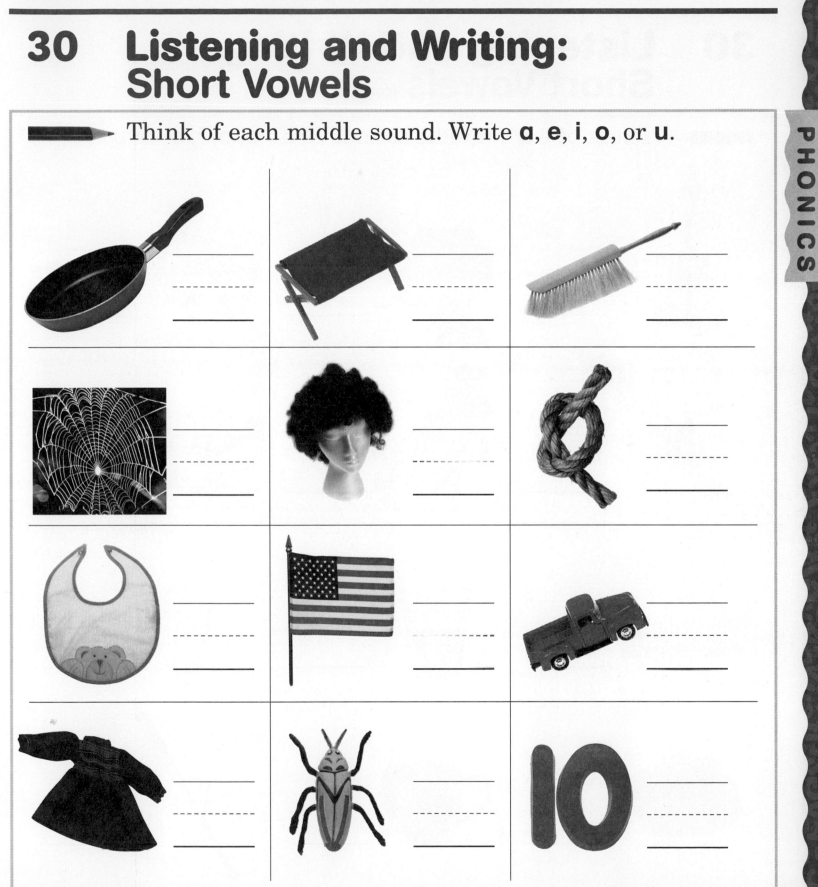

Skill: Children will write the letters that represent medial vowel sounds in picture names.

Home Activity: Say the words **met**, **tap**, **mix**, **run**, and **not**. After each word, ask your child to name the letter that spells the middle sound.

51

30 Listening and Writing: Short Vowels (continued)

Think of each middle sound. Write **a**, **e**, **i**, **o**, or **u**.

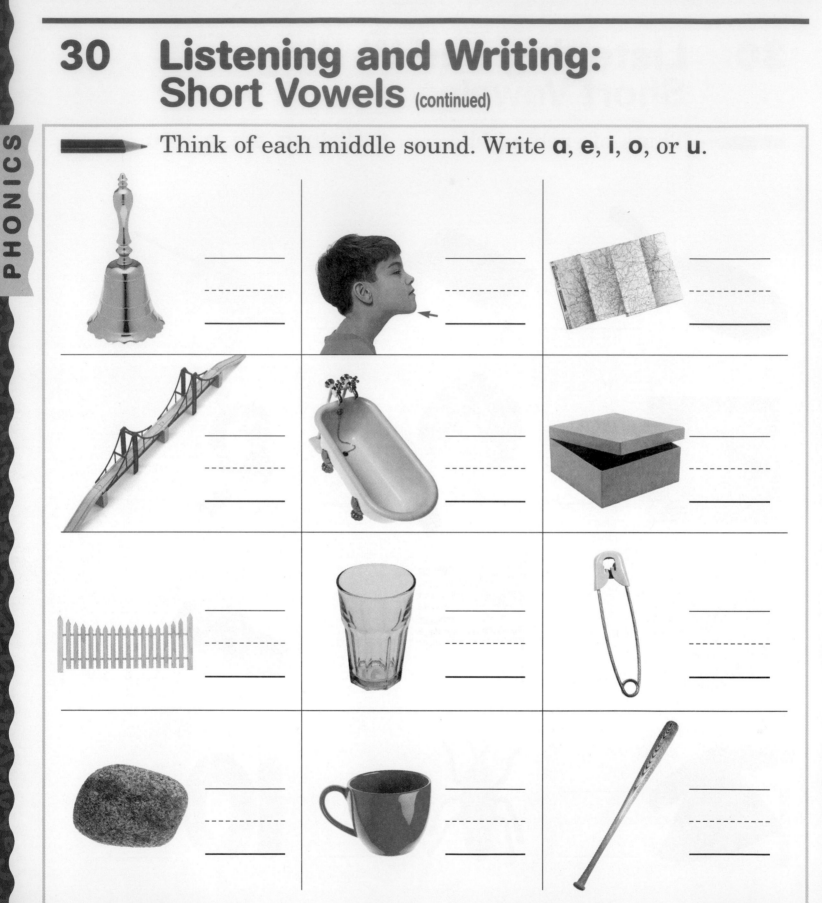

Skill: Children will write the letters that represent medial vowel sounds in picture names.

Home Activity: Draw simple pictures of the words **cup**, **bag**, **bed**, **clock**, and **ring**. Have your child write the letter that spells the middle sound in each picture name.

31 Listening and Writing: Short Vowels in Words

Think of each middle sound.
Write **a**, **e**, **i**, **o**, or **u** to spell each word.

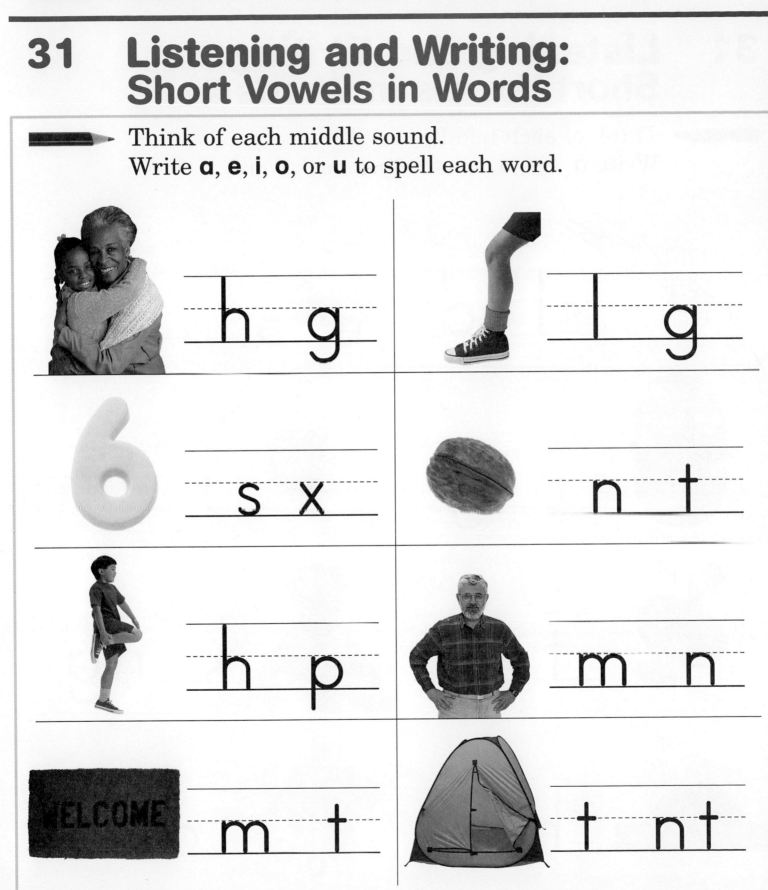

h __ g

l __ g

s __ x

n __ t

h __ p

m __ n

m __ t

t __ n t

Skill: Children will write medial vowels to complete words.

Home Activity: Read aloud the name for each picture on this page. After each word, ask your child to name the letter that spells the middle sound.

31 Listening and Writing: Short Vowels in Words (continued)

Think of each middle sound.
Write **a**, **e**, **i**, **o**, or **u** to spell each word.

s l __ d   v __ n

__ r g   l __ ck

t __ p   k __ ng

h __ ll   c __ t

Skill: Children will write medial vowels to complete words.

Home Activity: Say the first names **Bob, Jim, Bud, Beth,** and **Pat.** After each name, ask your child to name the letter that spells the middle sound.

Word List Units

Forest Friends

How to Study a Word

1 **LOOK** at the word.

- What letters spell the word?
- Name and touch each letter.

2 **SAY** the word.

- What sounds do you hear?
- How are the sounds spelled?

3 **THINK** about the word.

- Close your eyes and see the word.

4 **WRITE** the word.

- Think about the sounds and letters.
- Write each letter correctly.

5 **CHECK** the spelling.

- Are any letters missing?
- Are there any extra letters?

Spelling the 🍎 Sound

LOOK ⟩   SAY ⟩   THINK ⟩   WRITE ⟩   CHECK

1. **an**
2. **at**
3. **can**
4. **cat**
5. **had**
6. **man**

What letter spells the 🍎 sound?
Draw a line under this letter in each word you wrote.

Skill: Children will study the spellings of six words with the |ă| sound. They will write each word twice and will underline each vowel in the vowel-consonant pattern. **Picture clue: apple**

Home Activity: Have your child read, spell aloud, and trace with a finger each numbered word. Together, think of people's names that have the **apple** sound.

an	cat
at	had
can	man

Practice

✏️ Write the words that begin like the picture names.

1. _____

2. _____

3. _____

✏️ Write the two words that rhyme with 🏏.

4. _____

5. _____

✏️ Write the three words that rhyme with 🌀.

6. _____

7. _____

8. _____

Skill: Children will write spelling words that begin like and that rhyme with picture names.

Home Activity: With your child, review the spelling of each word on the list. Ask your child to name other words that rhyme with each spelling word.

Vocabulary Practice

an	cat
at	had
can	man

Write the missing words.

_____

1. Fox has pups _____ home.

_____

2. They tug on _____ old rag.

_____

3. They _____ to sleep today.

_____

4. We _____ take them out soon.

Write About a Pet Shop

Write a sentence about a pet shop.
Use **man** and **cat** in your sentence.

_____

_____

_____

_____

Skill: Children will write spelling words to complete sentences. They will write an original sentence, using two spelling words.

Home Activity: Have your child imagine what it would be like to own a pet shop. Ask your child to tell about the baby animals in the shop, using some of the spelling words.

an | cat
at | had
can | man

Writer's Dictionary

Write each spelling word under the correct letter in your Writer's Dictionary.

Review: Spelling Spree

Write the spelling word for each picture.

1.

2.

3.

Proofreading

Circle each spelling word that is wrong. Write it correctly.

_____

4. We have a pig et the farm. _____

_____

5. She hade one baby pig. _____

_____

6. They live in un open pen. _____

Skill: Children will complete a crossword puzzle by writing spelling words to match picture clues. They will circle misspelled spelling words and will write them correctly.

Home Activity: Give your child a practice spelling test. Say each spelling word aloud, and use it in a sentence. Have your child write each spelling word.

Special Words for Writing

| the | and | a |

Write the Special Words.

1. the

2. and

3. a

_____

_____

_____

_____

_____

_____

Write the missing Special Words.
Color the picture.

_____

4. Pat has _____ new bunny.

_____

5. It is soft _____ cute.

_____

6. It hops to _____ flowers.

Skill: Children will study the spellings of three high-frequency words. They will write each word in configuration boxes, in isolation, and in a sentence.

Home Activity: Ask your child to see how many times he or she can find the three Special Words on a printed page from a book, a newspaper, or a magazine.

Rhyming Words

Use the letters in the picture to make **at** words.

1. _____

2. _____

3. _____

4. _____

5. _____

6. _____

Copyright © Houghton Mifflin Company. All rights reserved.

Skill: Children will build new words by adding letters to a phonogram learned in this unit.

Home Activity: Discuss the picture with your child. Share something you know about baby animals, or together, read a book about this topic.

Name _____

Spelling the 🏠 Sound

LOOK SAY THINK WRITE CHECK

1. in
2. it
3. him
4. big
5. sit
6. did

What letter spells the 🏠 sound?
Draw a line under this letter in each word you wrote.

Skill: Children will study the spellings of six words with the [ĭ] sound. They will write each word twice and will underline each vowel in the vowel-consonant pattern. **Picture clue: igloo**

Home Activity: Have your child read, spell aloud, and trace with a finger each numbered word. Say additional words. Ask your child to clap after each word with the **igloo** sound.

in	big
it	sit
him	did

Practice

Write the word that begins like each picture name.

1. _____

2. _____

3. _____

4. _____

Write the two words that begin like 🏠 .

5. _____

6. _____

Write the two words that rhyme with 🧶 .

7. _____

8. _____

Skill: Children will write spelling words that begin like and that rhyme with picture names.

Home Activity: With your child, review the spelling of each word on the list. Ask your child to name other words that rhyme with each spelling word.

in	big
it	sit
him	did

Vocabulary Practice

✏ Write the missing words.

_____

1. We saw Pig _____ the band.

2. What _____ we see _____ play?

3. He played a _____ drum.

4. He had to _____ down.

Write About Music

📖 Write a sentence about a kind of music you like.
Use **it** in your sentence.

_____

_____

_____

_____

Skill: Children will write spelling words to complete sentences. They will write an original sentence, using one spelling word.

Home Activity: Ask your child to imagine that he or she has invented a new musical instrument. Have your child describe the instrument, using some of the spelling words.

in | big
it | sit
him | did

Writer's Dictionary

Write each spelling word under the correct letter in your Writer's Dictionary.

Review: Spelling Spree

Circle and write the hidden spelling words.

1. bdidg _____

2. ainpt _____

3. himog _____

4. svitp _____

Proofreading

Circle each spelling word that is wrong. Write it correctly.

5. Ann plays en the band. _____

6. She has a bic horn. _____

7. We sitt and watch. _____

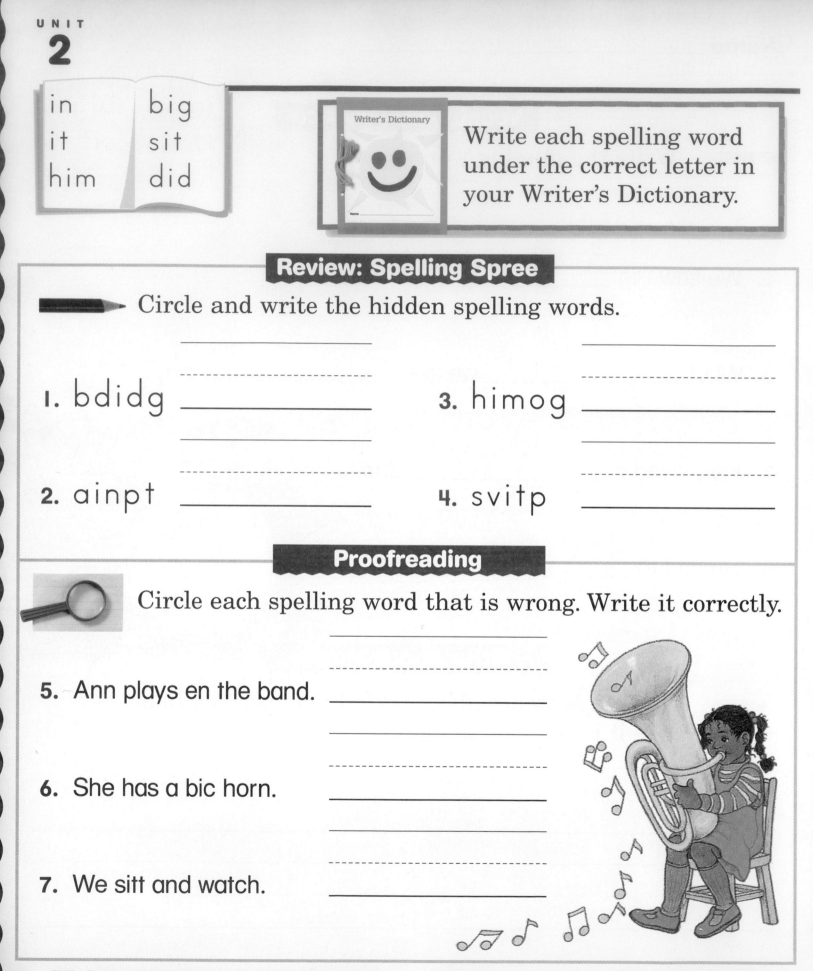

Skill: Children will find, circle, and write hidden spelling words. They will circle misspelled spelling words and will write them correctly.

Home Activity: Give your child a practice spelling test. Say each spelling word aloud, and use it in a sentence. Have your child write each spelling word.

Special Words for Writing

| to | of | is |

✏️ Write the Special Words.

1. to

2. of

3. is

✏️🖍️ Write the missing Special Words.
Color the picture.

4. I like _____ sing a lot.

5. This _____ my song book.

6. Two _____ the songs are new.

SING A SONG

Skill: Children will study the spellings of three high-frequency words. They will write each word in configuration boxes, in isolation, and in a sentence.

Home Activity: Ask your child to find the three Special Words in a magazine or a newspaper. Have your child cut out the words and paste them on a sheet of paper.

Rhyming Words

Use the letters in the picture to make six **ip** words.
Then write the **ip** words next to the correct picture.

1. _____

2. _____

3. _____

4. _____

5. _____

6. _____

PHONICS AND SPELLING

Skill: Children will build new words by adding letters to the **ip** phonogram.

Home Activity: Discuss the picture with your child. Share something you know about music, or together, read a book about this topic.

Name _____

3 Review: Units 1–2

Unit 1   Spelling the  Sound (pages 57–62)

> an   can   had
>
> at   cat   man

Write the two words that begin like 🍎 .

1. _____   2. _____

Write the missing words.

3. Do you see that tall _____ ?

4. He _____ four dogs.

5. Then he got a cute _____ .

6. How _____ he feed them all?

Skill: Children will write spelling words that begin with the |ă| sound. They will write spelling words to complete sentences.

Home Activity: Print several simple sentences on a sheet of paper. Misspell one spelling word in each sentence. Ask your child to find and correct the words that you misspelled.

3 Review

 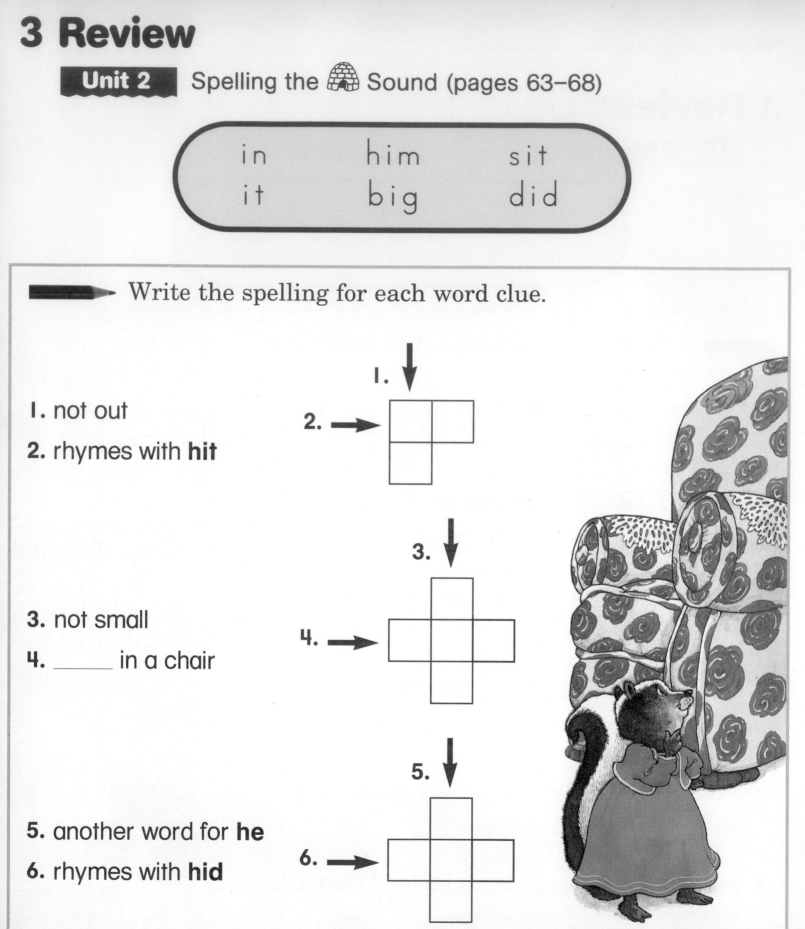

in	him	sit
it	big	did

Write the spelling for each word clue.

1. not out

2. rhymes with **hit**

3. not small

4. _____ in a chair

5. another word for **he**

6. rhymes with **hid**

1. ⬇

2. ➡

3. ⬇

4. ➡

5. ⬇

6. ➡

Skill: Children will complete crossword puzzles by writing spelling words to match printed clues.

Home Activity: Have your child give you a test on the spelling words. Print each word as your child reads it to you. Ask your child to correct your spelling test.

a b c d e f g h i j k l m n o p q r s t u v w x y z

Dictionary

Help Frog find the pond. Use ABC order.

Write the missing letters. Use ABC order.

a b ___ d ___ f g ___ i

j ___ l ___ n o ___ q r

s t ___ v ___ x y ___

Skill: Children will complete a maze by following letters in alphabetical order. They will write missing lowercase letters to complete the alphabet.

Home Activity: Slowly recite the alphabet, omitting certain letters. Ask your child to supply the missing letter each time you omit one.

Doghouse for Sale
by Donna Lugg Pape

Draw a picture of your room.

What else would you like to have in your room?
Add it to your drawing. Color your picture.

Skill: Children will listen to and then discuss a story. They will draw and revise a picture.

Home Activity: Have your child tell you about his or her drawing. Together, talk about another room in your home that you might like to change in some way.

Spelling the 🐙 Sound

LOOK ▷ SAY ▷ THINK ▷ WRITE ▷ CHECK

1. on

2. not

3. got

4. box

5. hot

6. top

✏️ What letter spells the 🐙 sound?
Draw a line under this letter in each word you wrote.

Skill: Children will study the spellings of six words with the |ŏ| sound. They will write each word twice and will underline each vowel in the vowel-consonant pattern. **Picture clue: octopus**

Home Activity: Have your child read, spell aloud, and trace with a finger each numbered word. Together, look through a store catalog for pictures whose names have the **octopus** sound.

on   box
not hot
got top

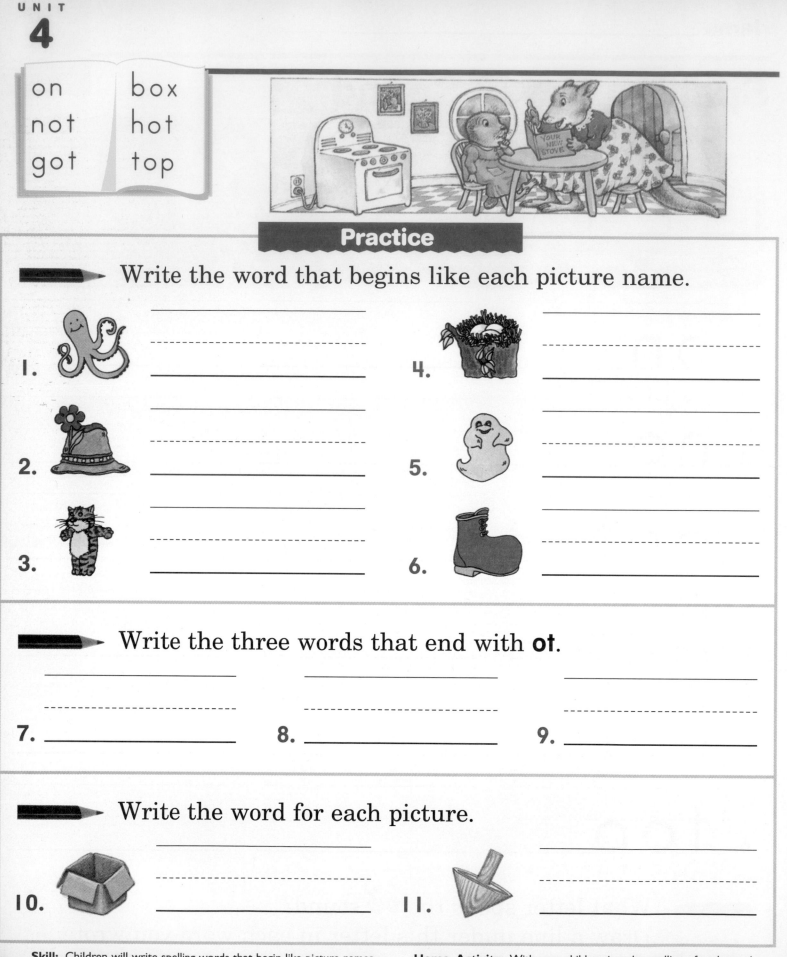

Practice

Write the word that begins like each picture name.

1. _____

2. _____

3. _____

4. _____

5. _____

6. _____

Write the three words that end with **ot**.

7. _____

8. _____

9. _____

Write the word for each picture.

10. _____

11. _____

Skill: Children will write spelling words that begin like picture names. They will write spelling words that end with the **ot** phonogram and that name pictured objects.

Home Activity: With your child, review the spelling of each word on the list. Together, make a list of other words that end with **op** and **ot**.

Vocabulary Practice

on | box
not | hot
got | top

Write the missing words.

_____

1. I have a first aid _____ .

_____   _____

2. I keep it _____ the _____ shelf.

_____

3. I _____ it from Owl.

_____

4. I hope I will _____ need it.

Write About Safety

Write a sentence about staying safe in your kitchen.
Use **hot** in your sentence.

_____

_____

_____

_____

Skill: Children will write spelling words to complete sentences. They will write an original sentence, using one spelling word.

Home Activity: With your child, write a few safety rules to follow in the kitchen. Use some spelling words in the rules. Post the list on the refrigerator.

on	box
not	hot
got	top

Write each spelling word under the correct letter in your Writer's Dictionary.

Review: Spelling Spree

Write the letter for each shape. Make spelling words.

h   n   t   o   b   x

1. _____

2. _____

3. _____

Proofreading

Circle each spelling word that is wrong. Write it correctly.

_____

4. The tob shelf was high.   _____

5. Bob did nawt climb up.   _____

6. Mom gut the glass for him.   _____

Skill: Children will use a code to write spelling words. They will circle misspelled spelling words and will write them correctly.

Home Activity: Give your child a practice spelling test. Say each spelling word aloud, and use it in a sentence. Have your child write each spelling word.

Special Words for Writing

| was | I | you |

✏️ Write the Special Words.

1. was

2. I

3. you

✏️ Write the missing Special Words.

4. Sue, did _____ find my skate?

5. Yes, _____ almost fell on it.

6. It _____ not in a safe place!

Skill: Children will study the spellings of three high-frequency words. They will write each word in configuration boxes, in isolation, and in a sentence.

Home Activity: Ask your child to find the three Special Words on cereal boxes, juice cartons, or other packages and containers in your kitchen.

Rhyming Words

Use the letters in the picture to make **ot** words.

1. _____

2. _____

3. _____

4. _____

5. _____

6. _____

Skill: Children will build new words by adding letters to a phonogram learned in this unit.

Home Activity: Discuss this picture with your child. Share something you know about home safety, or together, read a book about this topic.

Spelling the ◯ Sound

LOOK ⟩ SAY ⟩ THINK ⟩ WRITE ⟩ CHECK

1. get
2. ten
3. red
4. let
5. men
6. yes

What letter spells the ◯ sound?
Draw a line under this letter in each word you wrote.

Skill: Children will study the spellings of six words with the |ĕ| sound. They will write each word twice and will underline each vowel in the vowel-consonant pattern. **Picture clue: egg**

Home Activity: Have your child read, spell aloud, and trace with a finger each numbered word. Together, think of rhyming pairs of words that have the **egg** sound. *Example: red bed*

get | let
ten | men
red | yes

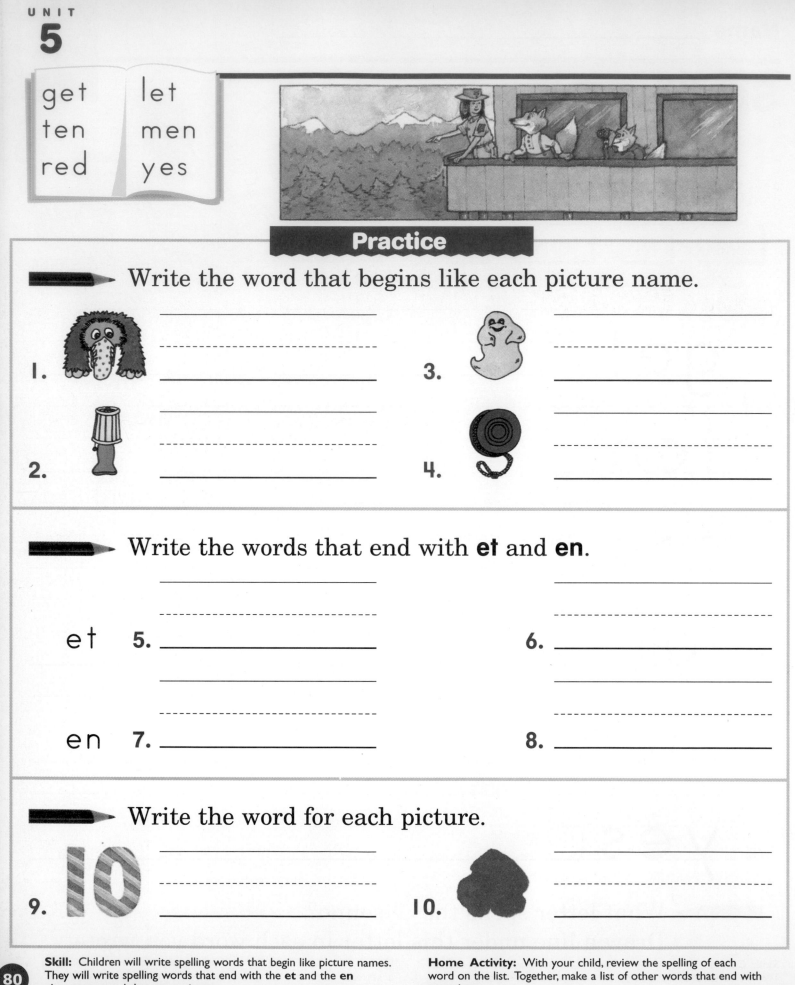

Practice

Write the word that begins like each picture name.

1. _____

2. _____

3. _____

4. _____

Write the words that end with **et** and **en**.

et 5. _____

6. _____

en 7. _____

8. _____

Write the word for each picture.

9. _____

10. _____

Skill: Children will write spelling words that begin like picture names. They will write spelling words that end with the **et** and the **en** phonograms and that name pictures.

Home Activity: With your child, review the spelling of each word on the list. Together, make a list of other words that end with **et** and **en**.

get   let
ten   men
red   yes

Vocabulary Practice

Write the missing words.

_____

1. Mom drives a _____ truck.

_____   _____

2. She works with _____ women and _____ .

_____

3. Will the cars _____ her go by?

_____

4. Oh _____ , she passes them.

Write About a Job

Write a sentence about a job you would like.
Use **get** in your sentence.

_____

_____

_____

_____

Skill: Children will write spelling words to complete sentences. They will write an original sentence, using one spelling word.

Home Activity: With your child, list some of the good things about the job he or she wrote about on this page. Try to use some of the spelling words.

81

get | let
ten | men
red | yes

Writer's Dictionary

Write each spelling word under the correct letter in your Writer's Dictionary.

Review: Spelling Spree

Add and take away letters. Write the spelling words.

1. $t + pen - p = ?$

2. $g + let - l = ?$

3. $y + best - b - t = ?$

1. _____

2. _____

3. _____

Proofreading

Circle each spelling word that is wrong. Write it correctly.

4. The min work hard. _____

5. One has a redd truck. _____

6. Will he lat me help? _____

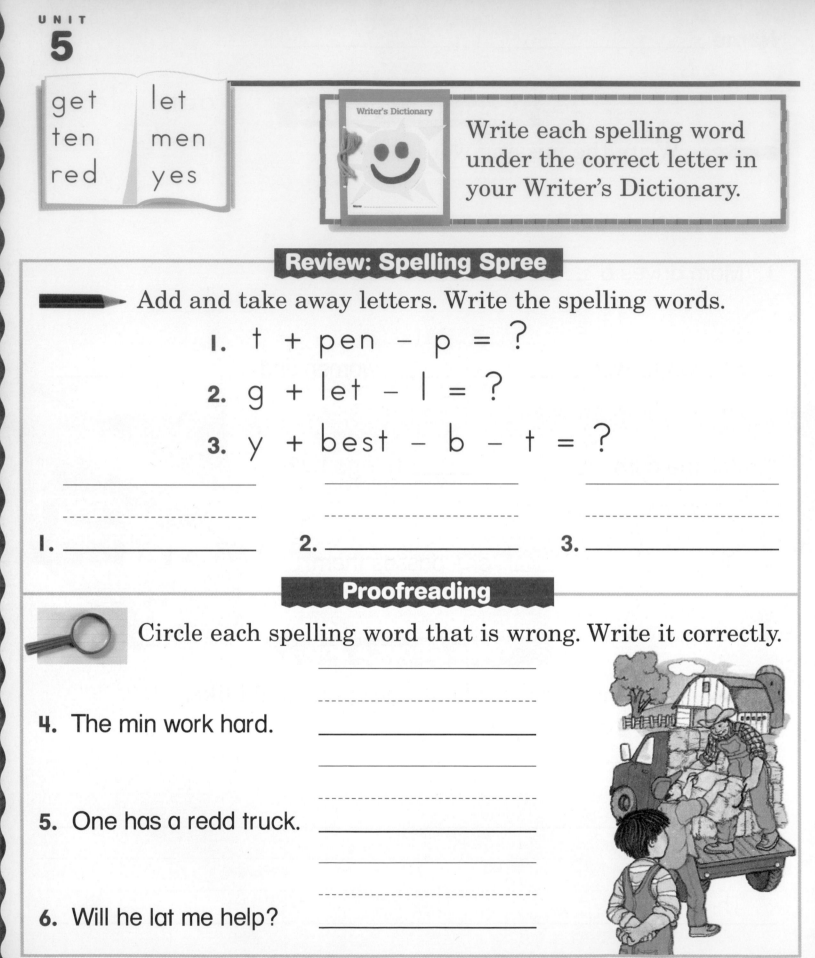

Skill: Children will add and subtract letters to write spelling words. They will circle misspelled spelling words and will write them correctly.

Home Activity: Give your child a practice spelling test. Say each spelling word aloud, and use it in a sentence. Have your child write each spelling word.

Special Words for Writing

| for | have | they |

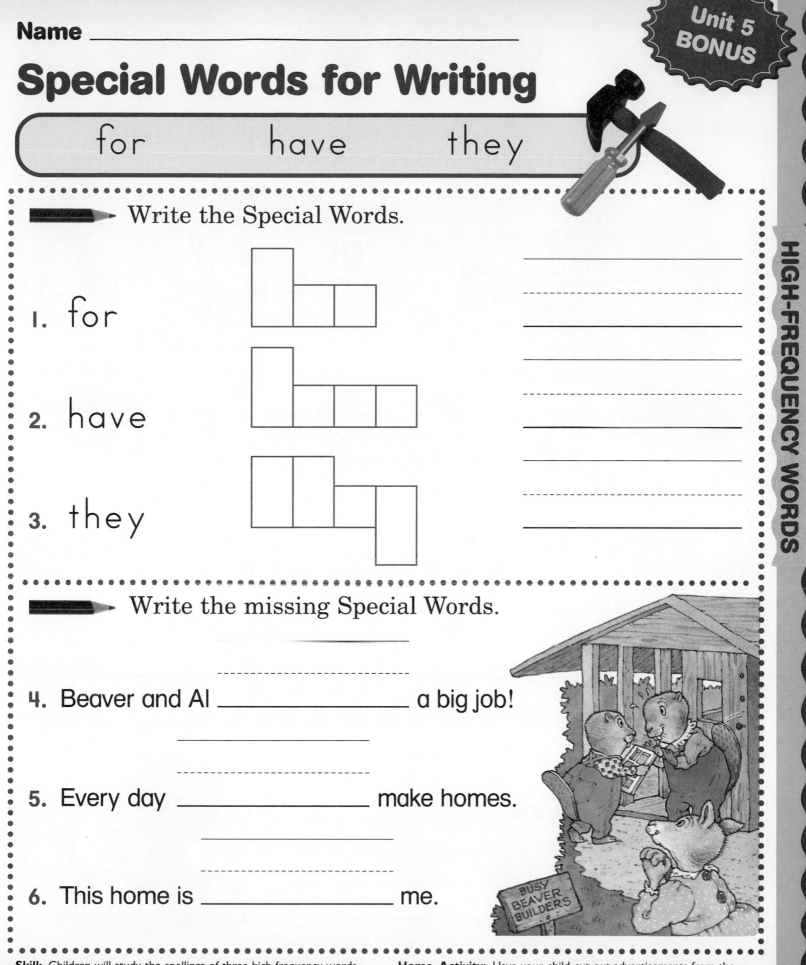

✏ Write the Special Words.

1. for

2. have

3. they

HIGH-FREQUENCY WORDS

✏ Write the missing Special Words.

4. Beaver and Al _____ a big job!

5. Every day _____ make homes.

6. This home is _____ me.

BUSY BEAVER BUILDERS

Skill: Children will study the spellings of three high-frequency words. They will write each word in configuration boxes, in isolation, and in a sentence.

Home Activity: Have your child cut out advertisements from the newspaper. Then ask your child to find and circle the three Special Words.

Rhyming Words

✏ Help find Max. Draw a path through the letters you can use to make **et** words.

Where are you, Max?

gr   y
vet   s
o   n
et   j   p   w   c

1. _____   3. _____   5. _____

2. _____   4. _____   6. _____

✏ Where is Max? Write an **et** word to finish each sentence.

7. He is not under the _____ .

8. Have you found him _____ ?

Skill: Children will build new words by adding letters to a phonogram learned in this unit.

Home Activity: Discuss this picture with your child. Share something you know about one career, or together, read a book about different careers.

PHONICS AND SPELLING

6 Review: Units 4–5

Unit 4   Spelling the 🐙 Sound (pages 73–78)

on	got	hot
not	box	top

✏️ Write **ot** in each box. Write the words.

1. g + ☐ = _____   2. h + ☐ = _____

✏️🖍️ Write the missing words.
Draw what you think is in the box.

_____

3. My gift is in a big _____ .

4. It has a flat _____ .

5. There is a bow _____ it.

6. I do _____ know what is inside!

Skill: Children will write spelling words that end with the **ot** phonogram. They will write spelling words to complete sentences.

Home Activity: On eight pieces of paper, print the letters **b, g, h, n, o, p, t,** and **x.** Say each spelling word. Have your child spell each word, using the paper letters.

6 Review

get red men
ten let yes

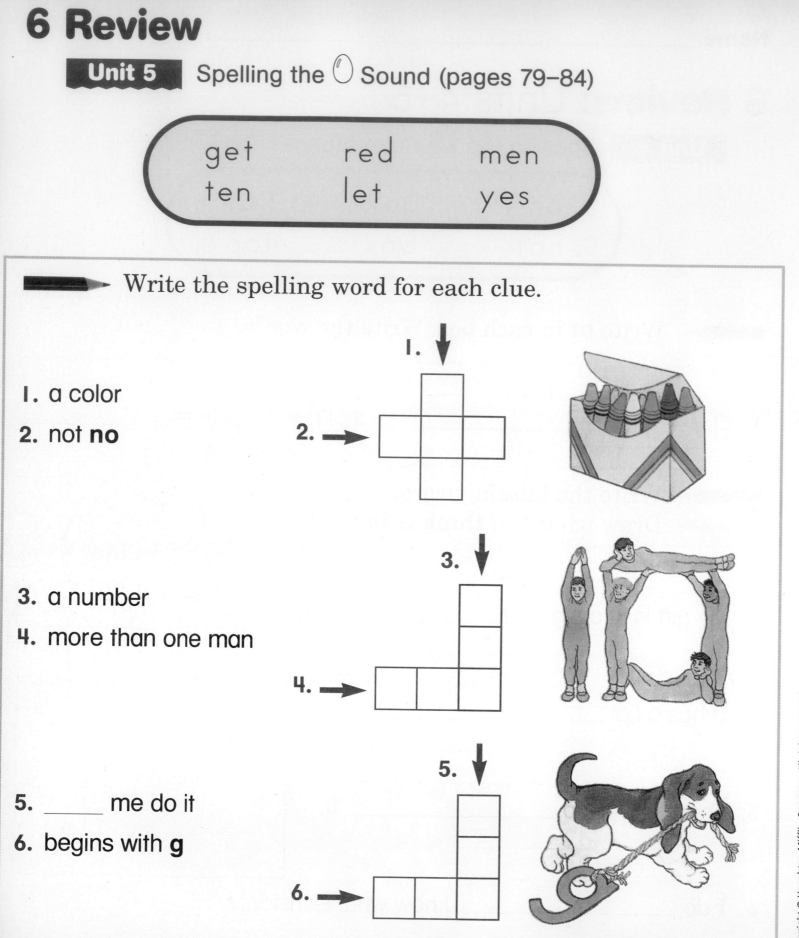

Write the spelling word for each clue.

1. a color
2. not **no**

3. a number
4. more than one man

5. _____ me do it
6. begins with **g**

Skill: Children will complete crossword puzzles by writing spelling words to match printed clues.

Home Activity: Provide your child with toothpicks, straws, or cotton swabs. Say each spelling word. Have your child form the letters in each word, using the chosen material.

Name _____

a b c d e f g h i j k l m n o p q r s t u v w x y z

Dictionary

Help Owl find her way home. Use ABC order.

Write the missing letters. Use ABC order.

1. j k ____ ____

2. a b ____ ____

3. s t ____ ____

4. m ____ ____ o

5. v ____ ____ x

6. ____ d ____ f

7. ____ ____ y z

8. ____ q r ____

9. ____ ____ h i

Skill: Children will complete a maze by following letters in alphabetical order. They will write letters to complete alphabetical letter groups.

Home Activity: Slowly recite the alphabet, periodically inserting incorrect letters. Ask your child to make a buzzing sound each time you make an error.

Dogs
by Marchette Chute

Draw a picture of your favorite pet.

What can you add to your drawing?
What can you change? Color your picture.

Skill: Children will listen to and then discuss a poem. They will draw, share, and revise a picture.

Home Activity: Have your child tell you about his or her drawing. Share something you know about pets, or together, read a book about choosing and raising a pet.

Spelling the ☂ Sound

LOOK ⟩ SAY ⟩ THINK ⟩ WRITE ⟩ CHECK

1. up _____

2. us _____

3. but _____

4. fun _____

5. cut _____

6. run _____

➤ What letter spells the ☂ sound?
Draw a line under this letter in each word you wrote.

Skill: Children will study the spellings of six words with the |ŭ| sound. They will write each word twice and will underline each vowel in the vowel-consonant pattern. **Picture clue: umbrella**

Home Activity: Have your child read, spell aloud, and trace with a finger each numbered word. Say additional words. Ask your child to jump after each word with the **umbrella** sound.

up	fun
us	cut
but	run

Practice

Write the word that begins like each picture name.

1. _____

2. _____

3. _____

4. _____

Write the two words that begin like ☂ .

5. _____

6. _____

Write the words that end with **ut** and **un**.

ut 7. _____

8. _____

un 9. _____

10. _____

Skill: Children will write spelling words that begin like picture names. They will write spelling words that end with the **ut** and the **un** patterns.

Home Activity: With your child, review the spelling of each word on the list. Together, make a list of other words that end with **ut** and **un**.

up   fun
us   cut
but   run

Vocabulary Practice

✏️ Write the missing words.
🖍️ Color the picture.

_____
- - - - - - - - - - - - -

1. Flying a kite was _____ .

_____
- - - - - - - - - - - - -

2. We had to _____ to make it fly.

_____
- - - - - - - - - - - - -

3. It flew, _____ it got stuck.

_____
- - - - - - - - - - - - -

4. We had to _____ the string.

Write About Things That Fly

📖 Write a sentence about something else that flies.
Use **us** and **up** in your sentence.

_____
- -

_____
- -

_____

Skill: Children will write spelling words to complete sentences. They will write an original sentence, using two spelling words.

Home Activity: Ask your child to pretend that he or she has invented something that can fly. Ask your child to tell about this invention, using some of the spelling words.

up	fun
us	cut
but	run

Writer's Dictionary

Write each spelling word under the correct letter in your Writer's Dictionary.

Review: Spelling Spree

Circle and write the hidden spelling words.

1. bbutw _____

2. runml _____

3. gtfun _____

4. ncutd _____

Proofreading

Circle each spelling word that is wrong. Write it correctly.

5. It must be fon to fly. _____

6. Birds fly yup in the sky. _____

7. Bugs fly around uz too. _____

Skill: Children will find, circle, and write hidden spelling words. They will circle misspelled spelling words and will write them correctly.

Home Activity: Give your child a practice spelling test. Say each spelling word aloud, and use it in a sentence. Have your child write each spelling word.

Name _____

Special Words for Writing

| are | one | all |

✏️ Write the Special Words.

1. are

2. one

3. all

✏️ Write the missing Special Words.

4. The bees _____ flying away.

5. Where do _____ of them live?

6. Each _____ lives in a hive.

Skill: Children will study the spellings of three high-frequency words. They will write each word in configuration boxes, in isolation, and in a sentence.

Home Activity: Ask your child to see how many times he or she can find the three Special Words on one or more pages of the customer guide in your telephone directory.

Rhyming Words

Use the letters in the picture to make **un** and **ut** words.

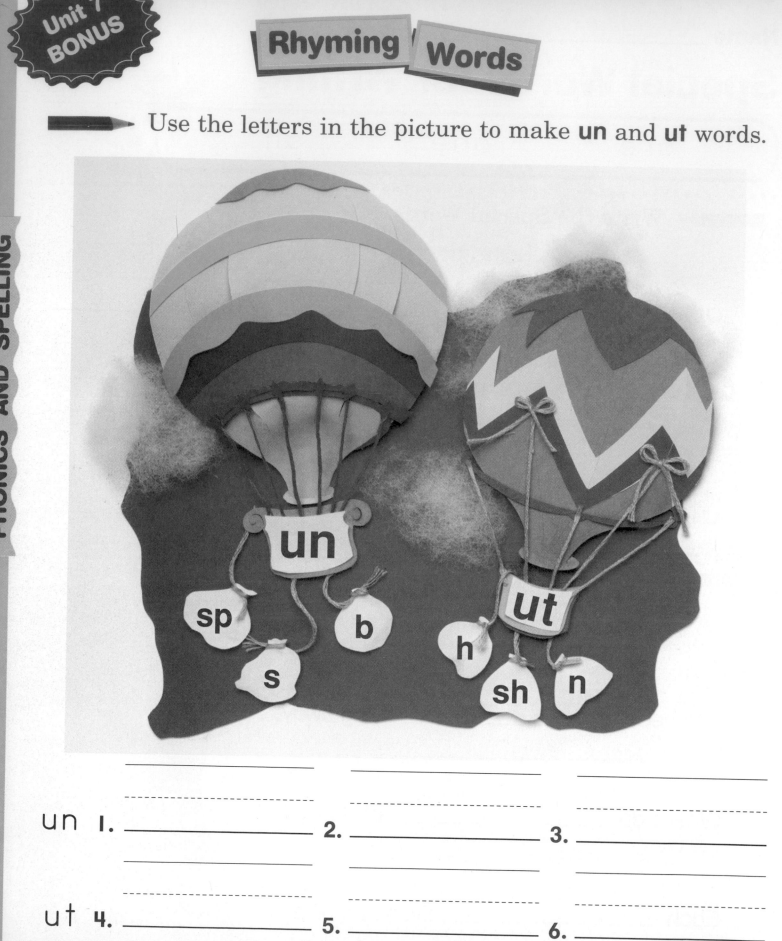

un **1.** _____ **2.** _____ **3.** _____

ut **4.** _____ **5.** _____ **6.** _____

Skill: Children will build new words by adding letters to phonograms learned in this unit.

Home Activity: Discuss the picture with your child. Share something you know about flight, or together read a book about this topic.

Spelling the 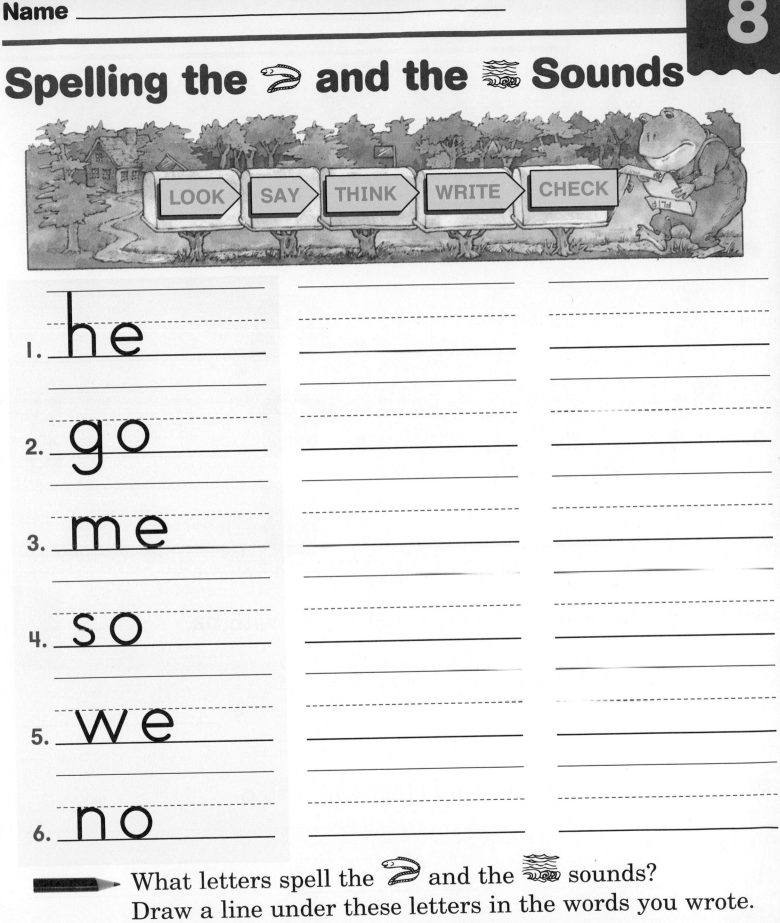 and the Sounds

LOOK ⟩ SAY ⟩ THINK ⟩ WRITE ⟩ CHECK

1. he

2. go

3. me

4. so

5. we

6. no

What letters spell the and the sounds?
Draw a line under these letters in the words you wrote.

Skill: Children will study six words with the |ē| or the |ō| sound. They will write each word twice and will underline each letter that spells the |ē| or the |ō| sound. **Picture clues: eel, ocean**

Home Activity: Have your child read, spell aloud, and trace with a finger each numbered word. Say each spelling word. Ask your child to clap after each word with the **eel** sound.

95

he	so
go	we
me	no

Practice

Write the word that begins like each picture name.

1. _____

2. _____

3. _____

4. _____

5. _____

6. _____

Write the three words that rhyme with **be**.

7. _____

8. _____

9. _____

Write the three words that end with **o**.

10. _____

11. _____

12. _____

Skill: Children will write spelling words that begin like picture names. They will write spelling words that rhyme with **be** and that end with **o**.

Home Activity: With your child, review the spelling of each word on the list. Together, make a list of other words that end with **o**. Examples: *radio, piano, hero*

Name _____

he	so
go	we
me	no

Vocabulary Practice

✏ Write the missing words.

_____

1. Fox showed _____ his car.

2. Then _____ and I drove _____ far!

3. It was hot, but _____ were cool.

4. There was _____ top on the car!

Write About a Trip

✏ Write a sentence about a funny car trip.
Use **go** in your sentence.

_____

_____

_____

_____

Skill: Children will write spelling words to complete sentences. They will write an original sentence, using one spelling word.

Home Activity: Have your child pretend that he or she is a famous race-car driver. Ask your child to tell about one of his or her races, using some of the spelling words.

he   so
go   we
me   no

Writer's Dictionary

Write each spelling word under the correct letter in your Writer's Dictionary.

Review: Spelling Spree

Write the spelling word for each clue.

1. not **stop**

2. not **yes**

3. another word for **us**

1. _____

2. _____

3. _____

Proofreading

Circle each spelling word that is wrong. Write it correctly.

4. This train is sow big. _____

5. Dad sits next to mee. _____

6. Soon hey and I will eat. _____

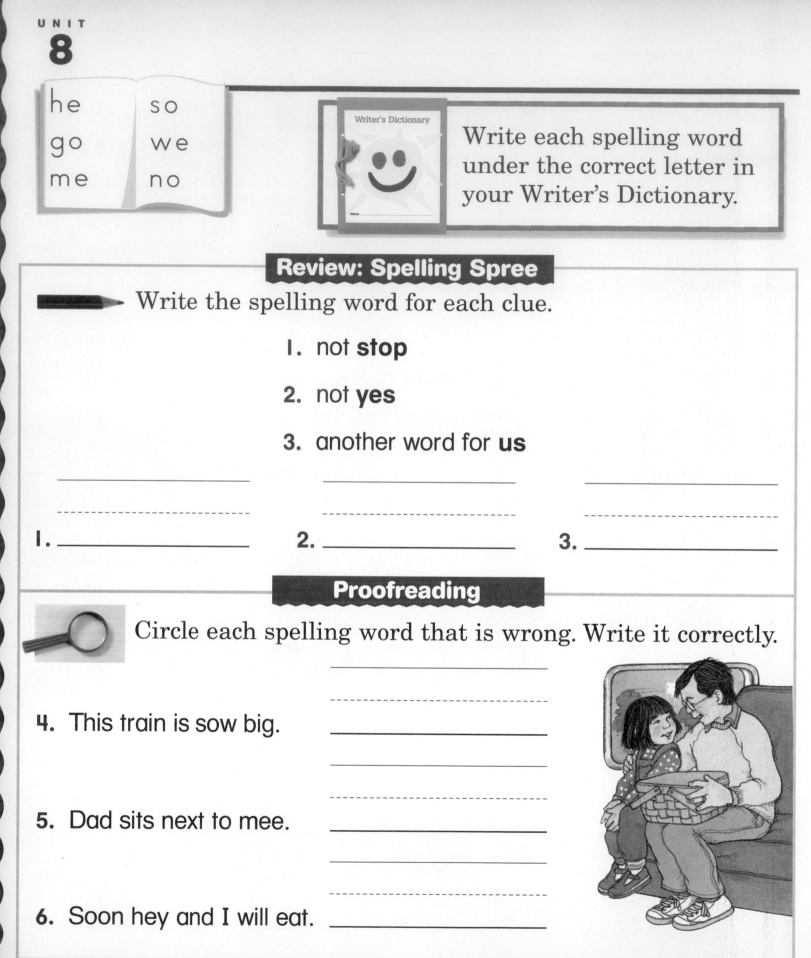

Skill: Children will write spelling words to match printed clues. They will circle misspelled spelling words and will write them correctly.

Home Activity: Give your child a practice spelling test. Say each spelling word aloud, and use it in a sentence. Have your child write each spelling word.

Name _____

Special Words for Writing

| there | his | as |

Write the Special Words.

1. there

2. his

3. as

Write the missing Special Words.
Color the picture.

4. Ted has _____ bus ticket.

5. The bus is over _____ .

6. We watch _____ he gets on.

Skill: Children will study the spellings of three high-frequency words. They will write each word in configuration boxes, in isolation, and in a sentence.

Home Activity: Ask your child to find and circle the three Special Words on a page from the Travel section of the newspaper.

Word Builder

✏️ Write **o** in each box. Then write the new words.

1. tomat + ☐ = _____

2. radi + ☐ = _____

3. pian + ☐ = _____

✏️ Use the words you made to finish this silly note.

4. _____

5. _____

6. _____

PHONICS AND SPELLING

Dear Uncle Cal,

We went for a little trip. We took a 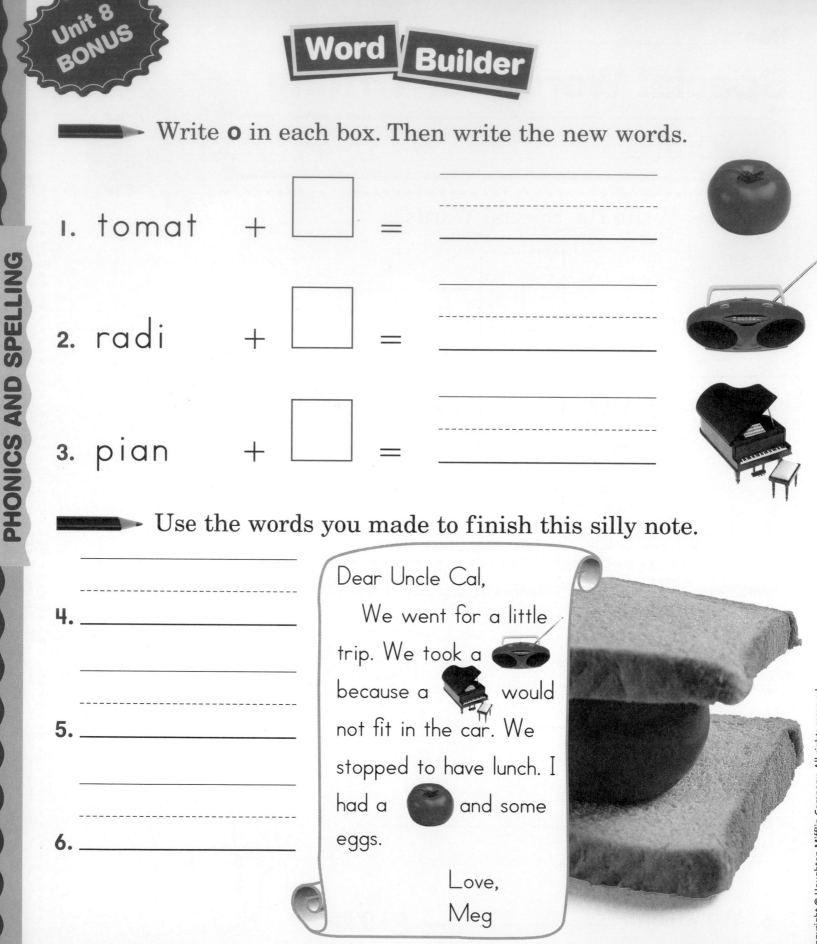 because a 🎹 would not fit in the car. We stopped to have lunch. I had a 🍅 and some eggs.

Love,
Meg

Skill: Children will build new words by adding **o** to other word parts. Then they will write the words and use those words to complete a rebus.

Home Activity: Discuss this page with your child. Share something you know about traveling, or together, read a book about taking a trip.

Name_____

9 Review: Units 7–8

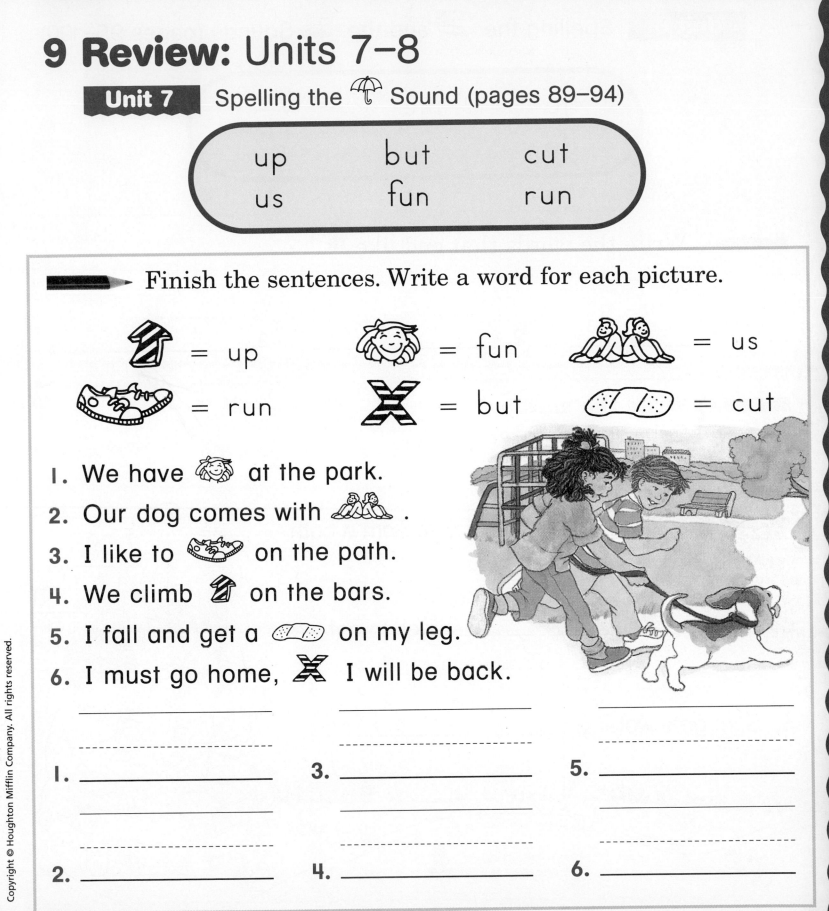

| Unit 7 | Spelling the ☂ Sound (pages 89–94) |

> up   but   cut
> us   fun   run

Finish the sentences. Write a word for each picture.

= up   = fun   = us

= run   = but   = cut

1. We have 😊 at the park.
2. Our dog comes with 👫 .
3. I like to 👟 on the path.
4. We climb ⬆ on the bars.
5. I fall and get a 🩹 on my leg.
6. I must go home, ✖ I will be back.

1. _____
2. _____
3. _____
4. _____
5. _____
6. _____

Skill: Children will complete sentences by writing spelling words to match picture clues.

Home Activity: Print each spelling word on a piece of heavy paper. Cut each word into two or three puzzle pieces. Have your child put the pieces together to make the spelling words.

9 Review

he	me	we
go	so	no

Write the words that end like 🎹 .

_____ _____ _____

1. _____ 2. _____ 3. _____

Write the missing words.
Color the picture.

_____

4. Today _____ give Sam a bath.

_____

5. I know _____ hates to get wet.

_____

6. Sam gets water on _____ !

Skill: Children will write spelling words that end with **o**. They will write spelling words to complete sentences.

Home Activity: Have your child give you a test on the spelling words. Print each word as your child reads it to you. Ask your child to correct your spelling test.

Name _____

a b c d e f g h i j k l m n o p q r s t u v w x y z

Dictionary

Draw a line from dot to dot. Use ABC order.

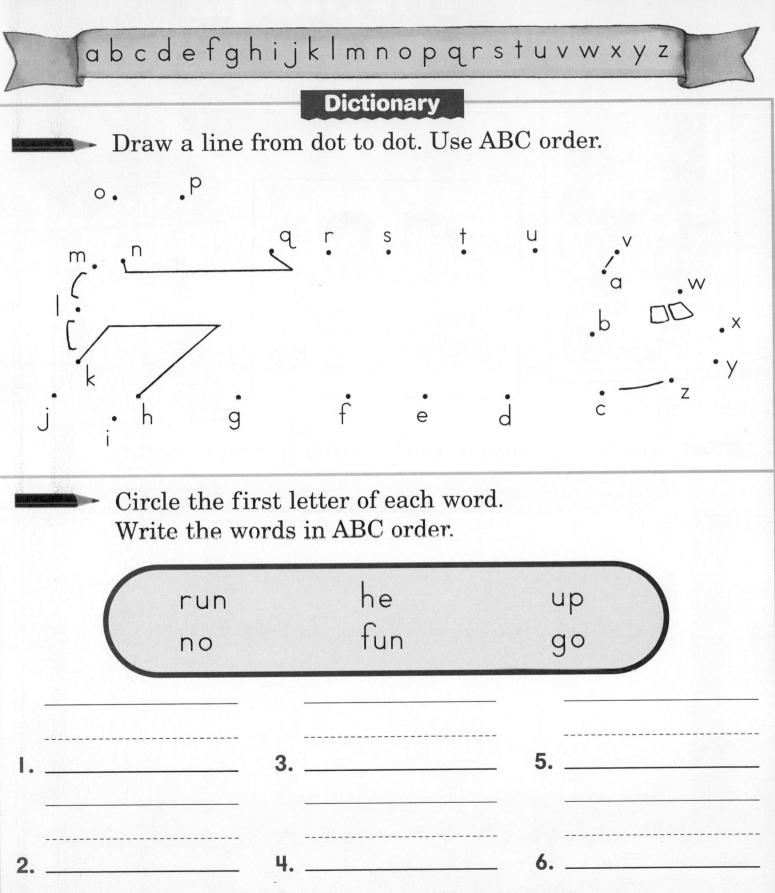

Circle the first letter of each word.
Write the words in ABC order.

run   he   up
no   fun   go

1. _____

2. _____

3. _____

4. _____

5. _____

6. _____

Skill: Children will connect dots in alphabetical order to complete a picture. They will alphabetize spelling words by the first letter.

Home Activity: Say pairs of animal names that begin with different letters. Ask your child to identify the word in each pair that comes first in ABC order.

Ira Sleeps Over
by Bernard Waber

Draw a picture of your favorite person to visit.

What can you add to your drawing?
What can you change? Color your picture.

Skill: Children will listen to and then discuss a story. They will draw, share, and revise a picture.

Home Activity: Have your child tell you about his or her drawing. Discuss with your child a special person or place you might visit together.

LITERATURE AND WRITING: My Favorite Visit

Spelling the 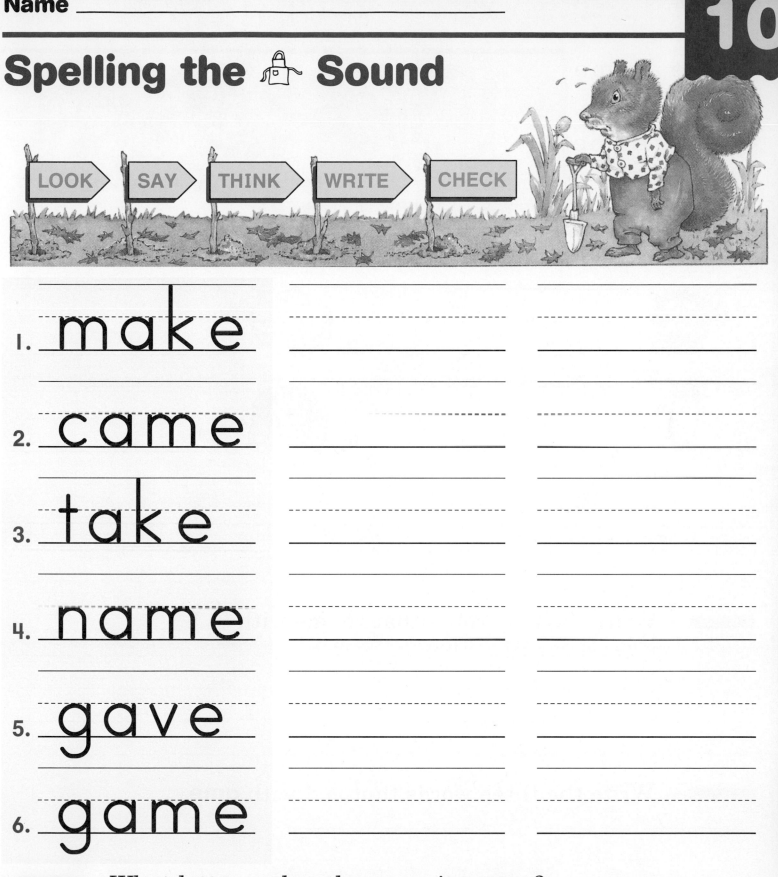 Sound

LOOK ▷ SAY ▷ THINK ▷ WRITE ▷ CHECK

1. make _____ _____

2. came _____ _____

3. take _____ _____

4. name _____ _____

5. gave _____ _____

6. game _____ _____

What letter makes the **a** say its name?
Draw a line under the last letter in each word you wrote.

Skill: Children will study six words with the |ā| sound spelled by the **a-consonant-e** pattern. They will write each word twice and will underline the final **e**. **Picture clue: apron**

Home Activity: Have your child read, spell aloud, and trace with a finger each numbered word. Say additional words. Ask your child to say "apron" after each word with the **apron** sound.

make name
came gave
take game

Practice

Write the words that begin like the picture names.

1. _____

2. _____

3. _____

4. _____

5. _____ _____

Write the two words that rhyme with 🎂 .

6. _____

7. _____

Write the three words that end with **ame**.

8. _____

9. _____

10. _____

Skill: Children will write spelling words that begin like and that rhyme with picture names. They will write spelling words that end with the **ame** pattern.

Home Activity: With your child, review the spelling of each word on the list. Together, make a list of other words that end with **ake** and **ame**.

Vocabulary Practice

make name
came gave
take game

Write the missing words.

_____

1. My friend's _____ is Jen.

2. She _____ here to _____ bread.

3. We will _____ the bread to Papa.

4. Then we will play a _____ .

Write About Something You Made

Write a sentence about something you made for someone. Use **gave** in your sentence.

_____

_____

_____

_____

Skill: Children will write spelling words to complete sentences. They will write an original sentence, using one spelling word.

Home Activity: Have your child use some of the spelling words to describe a special gift he or she would like to make for someone.

make	name
came	gave
take	game

Write each spelling word under the correct letter in your Writer's Dictionary.

Review: Spelling Spree

Write the letter for each shape. Make spelling words.

◇ t   ○ a   ▢ e   △ m   ♡ g   ☆ c   ▭ k

1. _____

2. _____

3. _____

Proofreading

Circle each spelling word that is wrong. Write it correctly.

4. Mom gaev me paper.   _____

5. I mak a hat with it.   _____

6. I put my nam on my hat.   _____

Skill: Children will use a code to write spelling words. They will circle misspelled spelling words and will write them correctly.

Home Activity: Give your child a practice spelling test. Say each spelling word aloud, and use it in a sentence. Have your child write each spelling word.

Special Words for Writing

were   would   out

✏️ Write the Special Words.

_____

1. were

_____

2. would

_____

3. out

_____

✏️🖍️ Write the missing Special Words.
Color the picture.

_____

4. Squirrel went _____ for food.

_____

5. Nuts _____ hard to find.

_____

6. How _____ his friends help him?

Skill: Children will study the spellings of three high-frequency words. They will write each word in configuration boxes, in isolation, and in a sentence.

Home Activity: Pour some salt or sand into a small box or tin. Have your child write each Special Word in the salt or the sand with a finger. Shake the box gently to erase each word.

Rhyming Words

Use the letters in the picture to make **ake** words.

ake

sh   fl

c

r

l   b

1. _____
2. _____
3. _____

4. _____
5. _____
6. _____

Tell how to make a cake. Use an **ake** word.

_____
_____
_____
_____
_____

PHONICS AND SPELLING

110

Skill: Children will build new words by adding letters to a phonogram learned in this unit. They will write a sentence using an **ake** word.

Home Activity: Discuss the picture with your child. Share something you know about a particular craft, or together, read a "how to" book.

Spelling the  Sound

LOOK SAY THINK WRITE CHECK

1. like _____ _____

2. five _____ _____

3. ride _____ _____

4. nine _____ _____

5. time _____ _____

6. bike _____ _____

What letter makes the **i** say its name?
Draw a line under the last letter in each word you wrote.

Skill: Children will study six words with the |ī| sound spelled by the
i-consonant-**e** pattern. They will write each word twice and will
underline the final **e**. **Picture clue: ice**

Home Activity: Have your child read, spell aloud, and trace with a
finger each numbered word. Say additional words. Ask your child to
say "ice" after each word with the **ice** sound.

like   nine
five   time
ride   bike

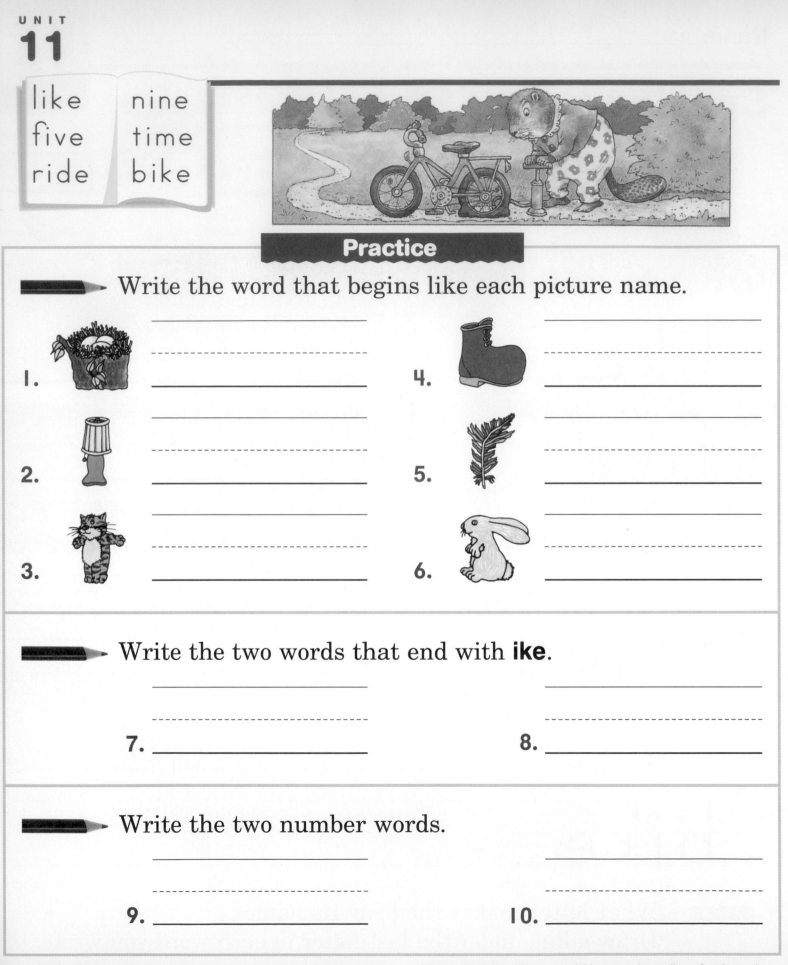

Practice

Write the word that begins like each picture name.

1. _____

2. _____

3. _____

4. _____

5. _____

6. _____

Write the two words that end with **ike**.

7. _____   8. _____

Write the two number words.

9. _____   10. _____

Skill: Children will write spelling words that begin like picture names. They will write spelling words that end with the **ike** pattern and that name numbers.

Home Activity: With your child, review the spelling of each word on the list. Together, make a list of other words that end with **ide** and **ine**.

Vocabulary Practice

like   nine
five   time
ride   bike

Write the missing words.

_____

_____

1. I have a new red _____ .

_____   _____

_____   _____

2. I _____ to _____ it all day.

_____

_____

3. I take _____ animals with me.

_____

_____

4. We have a good _____ .

Write About a Bike Store

Write a sentence about a trip to a bike store.
Use **nine** in your sentence.

_____

_____

_____

_____

_____

Skill: Children will write spelling words to complete sentences. They will write an original sentence, using one spelling word.

Home Activity: Have your child pretend that he or she owns a special bicycle. Ask your child to describe this special bicycle, using some of the spelling words.

113

like nine
five time
ride bike

Write each spelling word under the correct letter in your Writer's Dictionary.

Writer's Dictionary

Review: Spelling Spree

Write the spelling word for each picture.

1. 9

2. 5

3.

Proofreading

Circle each spelling word that is wrong. Write it correctly.

4. I love my new bik! _____

5. I really lyke to ride. _____

6. I ride all the tine. _____

NO PARKING

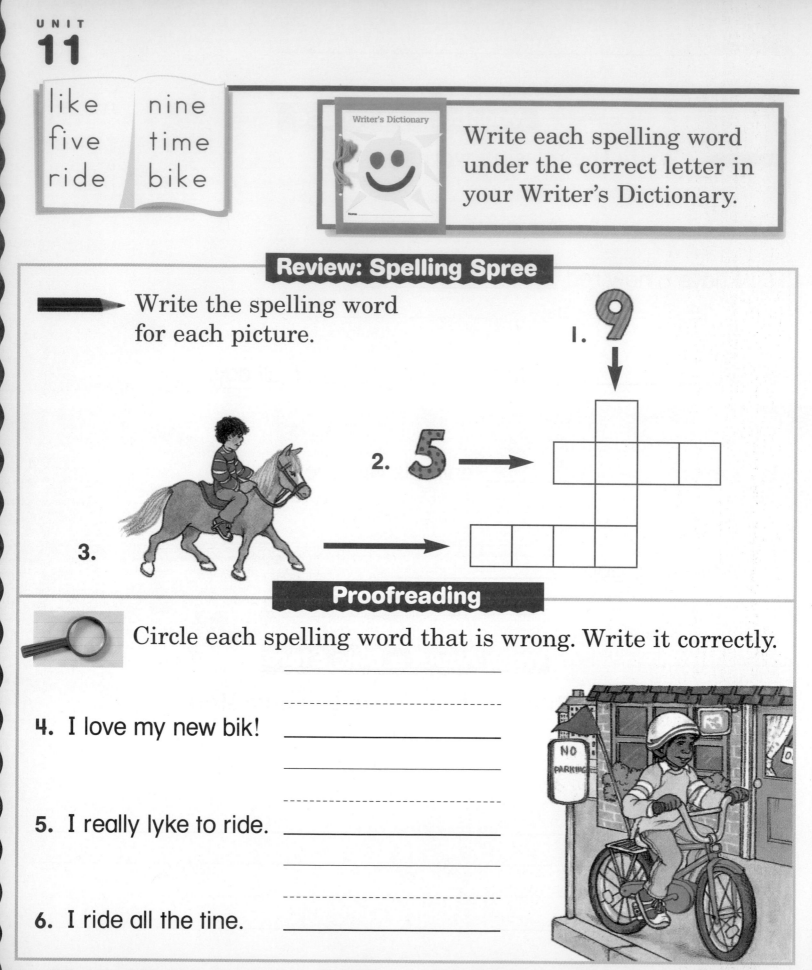

Skill: Children will complete a crossword puzzle by writing spelling words to match picture clues. They will circle misspelled spelling words and will write them correctly.

Home Activity: Give your child a practice spelling test. Say each spelling word aloud, and use it in a sentence. Have your child write each spelling word.

Special Words for Writing

from   will   do

HIGH-FREQUENCY WORDS

Write the Special Words.

1. from

2. will

3. do

_____
- - - - - - - - - - - - - - -
_____
- - - - - - - - - - - - - - -
_____
- - - - - - - - - - - - - - -
_____

Write the missing Special Words.
Color the picture.

_____
- - - - - - - - - -
4. I got a new bike _____ Owl.

_____
- - - - - - - - - -
5. She shows me what to _____ .

_____
- - - - - - - - - -
6. I _____ be a good rider soon!

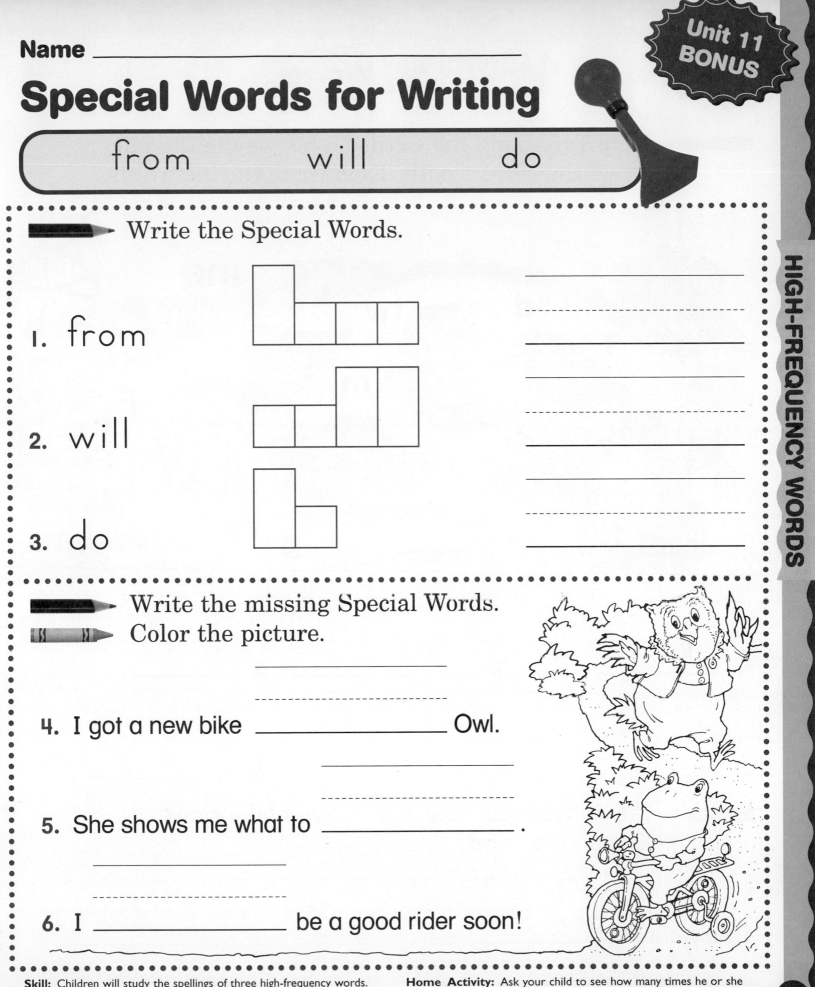

Skill: Children will study the spellings of three high-frequency words. They will write each word in configuration boxes, in isolation, and in a sentence.

Home Activity: Ask your child to see how many times he or she can find the three Special Words on a printed page from a toy catalog or a magazine.

Rhyming Words

Help Taro build **ine** words on his way to the fair. Draw the correct path. Then write the **ine** words.

1. _____

2. _____

3. _____

4. _____

5. _____

6. _____

Finish this sentence about Taro's bike ride. Use an **ine** word.

Taro went past _____ .

Skill: Children will build new words by adding letters to a phonogram learned in this unit. They will write a sentence using an **ine** word.

Home Activity: Discuss the picture with your child. Share something you know about bicycles, or together, read a book about this topic.

12 Review: Units 10–11

Unit 10   Spelling the 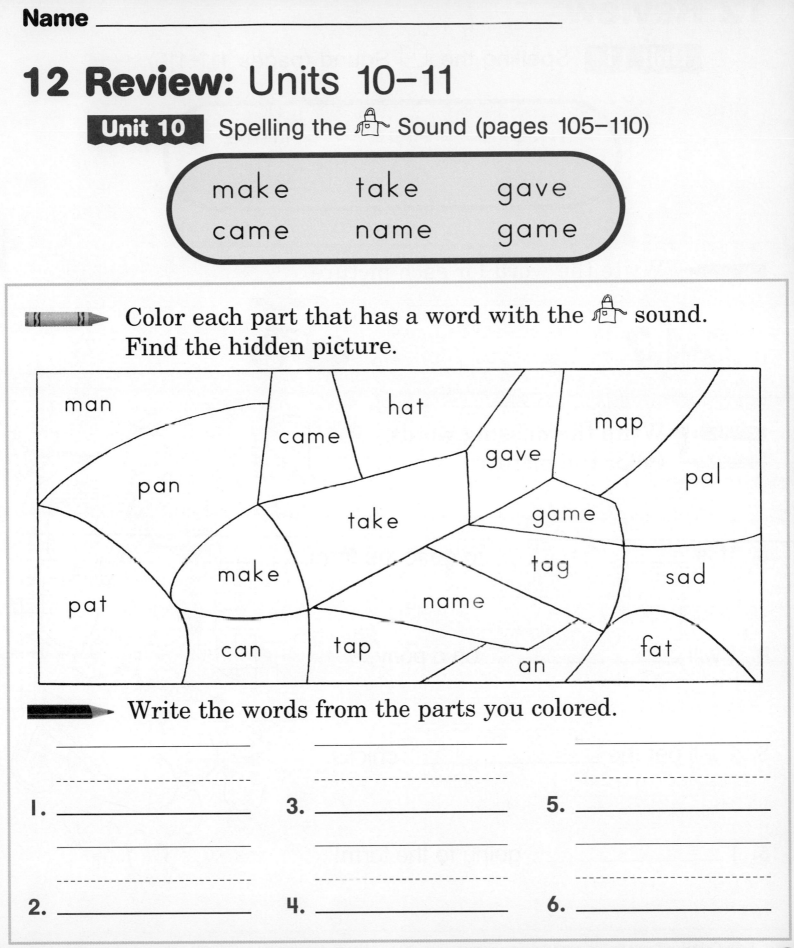 Sound (pages 105–110)

> make   take   gave
>
> came   name   game

Color each part that has a word with the 🛍 sound.
Find the hidden picture.

man	hat · map
came	gave · pal
pan	
take	game
make	tag · sad
pat	name
can · tap	an · fat

Write the words from the parts you colored.

1. _____

2. _____

3. _____

4. _____

5. _____

6. _____

Skill: Children will find a hidden picture by coloring shapes containing spelling words with the |ā| sound. They will write each spelling word.

Home Activity: Make dough by combining two cups of flour with one cup each of salt and water. Say each spelling word. Have your child use the dough to form the letters in each word.

12 Review

> like   ride   time
> five   nine   bike

✏️ Write the word for each picture.

1. 8+1=? _____

2. _____

✏️ Write the missing words.
🖍 Color the picture.

3. It is _____ to go to the farm.

4. I will _____ on a pony.

5. I will pet the _____ chicks.

6. I _____ going to the farm!

Skill: Children will write spelling words that name pictures. They will write spelling words to complete sentences.

Home Activity: Have your child cut the letters **b, d, e, f, i, k, l, m, r, t, v,** and two **n**'s from newspaper or magazine headlines. Have your child use the letters to spell each word.

a b c d e f g h i j k l m n o p q r s t u v w x y z

Dictionary

✏️ Draw a line from dot to dot. Use ABC order.

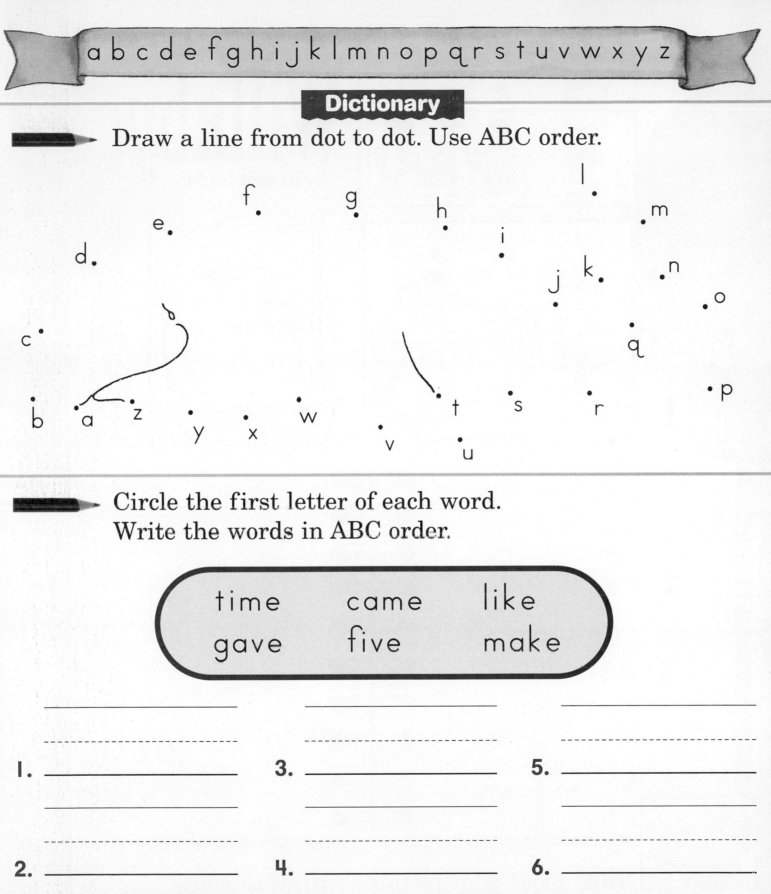

✏️ Circle the first letter of each word.
Write the words in ABC order.

> time   came   like
> gave   five   make

1. _____

2. _____

3. _____

4. _____

5. _____

6. _____

Skill: Children will connect dots in alphabetical order to complete a picture. They will alphabetize spelling words by the first letter.

Home Activity: Say random pairs of letters. Ask your child to identify the letter in each pair that comes first in ABC order.

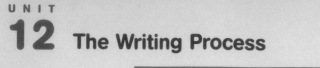

Willaby
by Rachel Isadora

Draw two pictures of things your class has done together.

Talk about your pictures with your class.

Skill: Children will listen to and then discuss a story about a class activity. They will generate topic ideas by drawing and will participate in writing a class story.

Home Activity: Have your child tell you about his or her drawing. Share something you remember about your school days, or together, read the book **Miss Nelson is Missing!** by Harry Allard.

Words Spelled with cl, fl, or sl

LOOK ▷ SAY ▷ THINK ▷ WRITE ▷ CHECK

1. clap _____ _____

2. sled _____ _____

3. flag _____ _____

4. club _____ _____

5. flat _____ _____

6. slip _____ _____

What are the sounds of **cl**, **fl**, and **sl**?
Draw a line under **cl**, **fl**, or **sl** in each word you wrote.

Skill: Children will study the spellings of six words that begin with the consonant cluster **cl, fl,** or **sl.** They will write each word twice and will underline **cl, fl,** or **sl.**

Home Activity: Have your child read, spell aloud, and trace with a finger each numbered word. Say each spelling word. Ask your child to name the first two letters in each word.

clap | club
sled | flat
flag | slip

Practice

Write the words that begin with **cl** and **sl**.

cl
1. _____ 2. _____

sl
3. _____ 4. _____

Write the three words with the 🍎 sound.

5. _____ 6. _____ 7. _____

Write the word for each picture.

8. _____

9. _____

10. _____

Skill: Children will write spelling words that begin with **cl** and **sl**. They will write spelling words that have the |ă| sound and that name pictures.

Home Activity: With your child, review the spelling of each word on the list. Together, make a list of other words that begin with **cl**, **fl**, and **sl**.

clap	club
sled	flat
flag	slip

Vocabulary Practice

➤ Write the missing words.

_____

1. Will you be in our _____ ?

2. We _____ loudly and wave a _____ .

3. We sit on a long, _____ bench.

4. We try not to _____ on the ice.

Write About Winter Fun

Write a sentence about another kind of fun thing to do in the winter. Use **sled** in your sentence.

_____

_____

_____

_____

Skill: Children will write spelling words to complete sentences. They will write an original sentence, using one spelling word.

Home Activity: Have your child pretend that he or she is a sports reporter. Ask your child to describe a winter sport, using some of the spelling words.

clap | club
sled | flat
flag | slip

Writer's Dictionary

Name

Write each spelling word under the correct letter in your Writer's Dictionary.

Review: Spelling Spree

Write the spelling word for each clue.

1. You ride on this in the snow.
2. You do this with both hands.
3. It may be red, white, and blue.

1. _____   2. _____   3. _____

Proofreading

Circle each spelling word that is wrong. Write it correctly.

_____

4. Our klub plays outside. _____

_____

5. We skate on the flet ice. _____

_____

6. I silp and fall down. _____

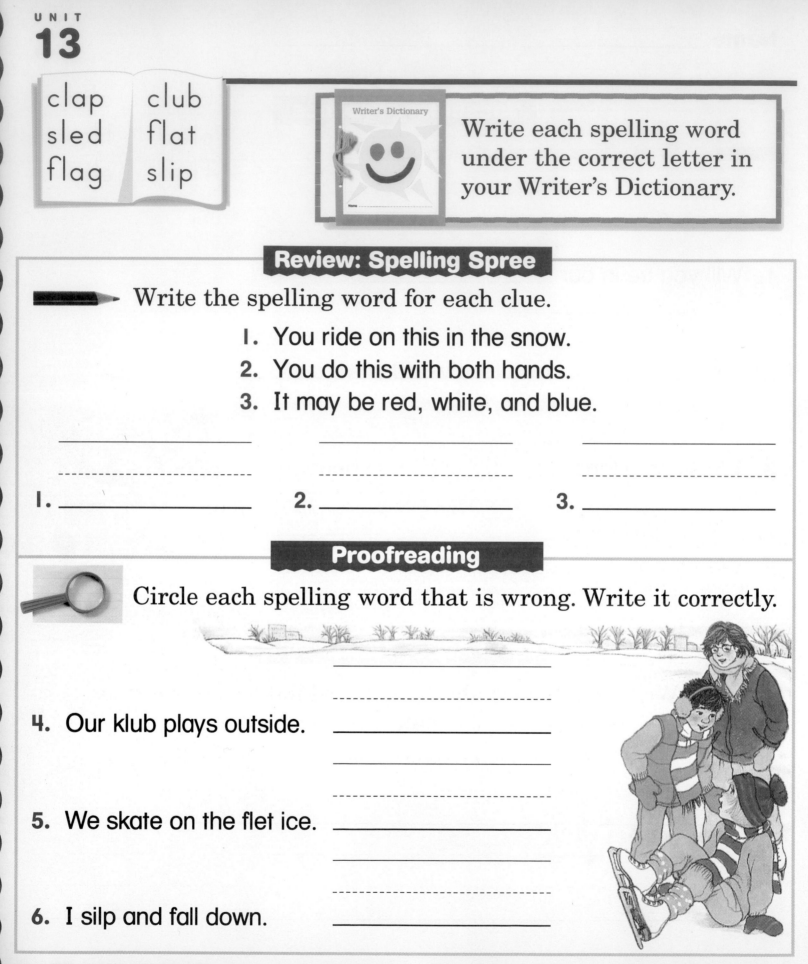

Skill: Children will write spelling words to match printed clues. They will circle misspelled spelling words and will write them correctly.

Home Activity: Give your child a practice spelling test. Say each spelling word aloud, and use it in a sentence. Have your child write each spelling word.

Special Words for Writing

| said | what | her |

✏️ Write the Special Words.

1. said

_____

2. what

_____

3. her

_____

✏️🖍️ Write the missing Special Words.
Color the picture.

_____

4. Mom _____ she loves the snow.

_____

5. I go up the hill with _____ .

_____

6. She shows me _____ to do.

Skill: Children will study the spellings of three high-frequency words. They will write each word in configuration boxes, in isolation, and in a sentence.

Home Activity: Ask your child to find the three Special Words in a magazine or a newspaper. Have your child cut out the words and paste them on this page.

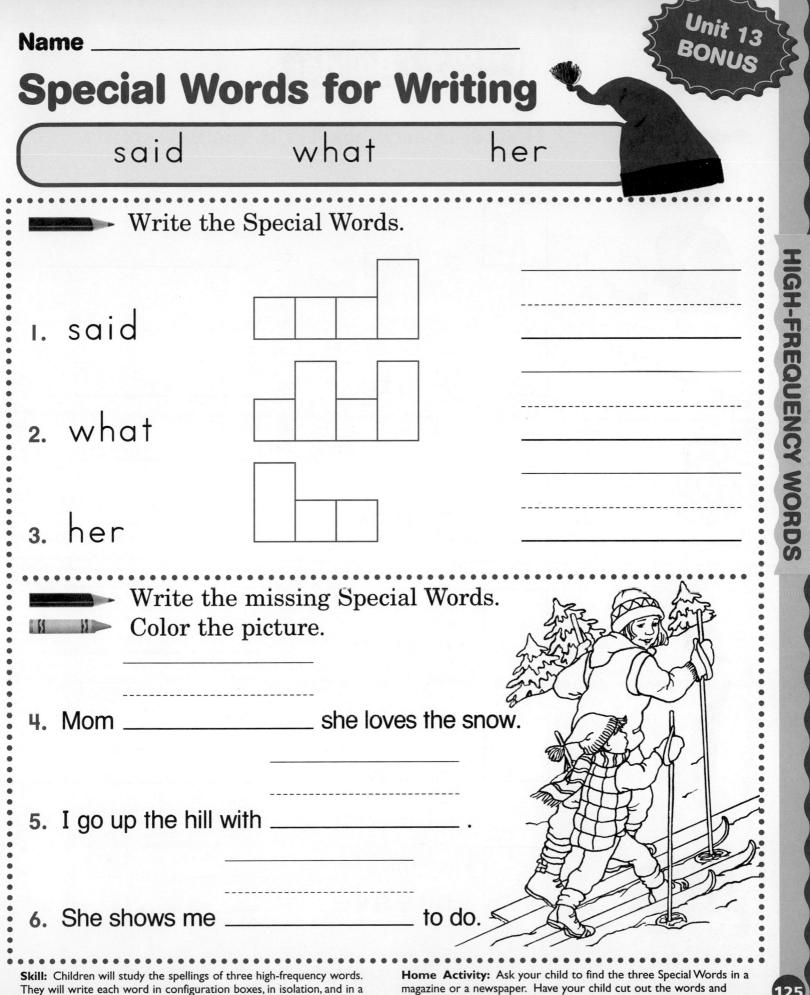

Word Builder

Write **cl**, **fl**, or **sl** in each box. Write the new words.

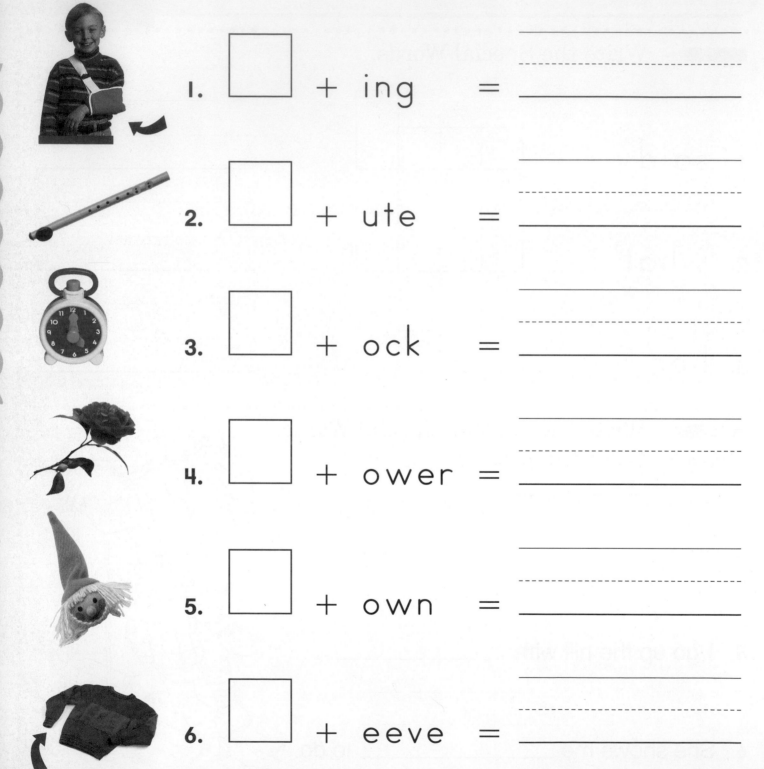

1. ☐ + ing = _____

2. ☐ + ute = _____

3. ☐ + ock = _____

4. ☐ + ower = _____

5. ☐ + own = _____

6. ☐ + eeve = _____

Skill: Children will build new words by adding **cl**, **fl**, or **sl** to other word parts.

Home Activity: Say aloud some words that begin with **cl**, **fl**, or **sl** and ask your child to tell you what two letters start each word.

Name _____

Spelling the  Sound with e e

LOOK > SAY > THINK > WRITE > CHECK

1. see _____ _____

2. keep _____ _____

3. green _____ _____

4. feet _____ _____

5. bee _____ _____

6. sleep _____ _____

What two letters spell the 🐟 sound?
Draw a line under these letters in each word you wrote.

Skill: Children will study the spelling of six words with the |ē| sound. They will write each word twice and will underline the letters that spell the |ē| sound. **Picture clue: eel**

Home Activity: Have your child read, spell aloud, and trace with a finger each numbered word. Say additional words. Ask your child to say "eel" after each word with the **eel** sound.

see | feet
keep | bee
green | sleep

Practice

➤ Write the word that begins like each picture name.

1. _____

2. _____

3. _____

➤ Write the two words that rhyme with 3.

4. _____

5. _____

➤ Write the word for each picture.

6. _____

7. _____

8. _____

Skill: Children will write spelling words that begin like and that rhyme with picture names. They will write spelling words that name pictures.

Home Activity: With your child, review the spelling of each word on the list. Together, make a list of other words spelled with **ee.**

see | feet
keep | bee
green | sleep

Vocabulary Practice

➤ Write the missing words.

_____

1. A _____ is in my garden.

2. I _____ it land by my _____ .

3. Please _____ it away from me.

4. I hope it goes to _____ !

Write About a Garden

✏ Write a sentence about a special garden.
Use **green** in your sentence.

_____

_____

_____

_____

Skill: Children will write spelling words to complete sentences. They will write an original sentence, using one spelling word.

Home Activity: Have your child pretend that he or she has a garden. Ask your child to tell about what he or she does in the garden, using some of the spelling words.

see   feet
keep   bee
green sleep

Writer's Dictionary

Name _____

Write each spelling word under the correct letter in your Writer's Dictionary.

Review: Spelling Spree

Circle and write the hidden spelling words.

b b e e d t   e s l e e p   t f e e t h

_____   _____   _____

- - - - - - - - - -   - - - - - - - - - -   - - - - - - - - - -

1. _____   2. _____   3. _____

Proofreading

Circle each spelling word that is wrong. Write it correctly.

_____

- - - - - - - - - -

4. Do you se my garden?   _____

_____

- - - - - - - - - -

5. I keap weeds out of it.   _____

_____

- - - - - - - - - -

6. Every leaf is grene.   _____

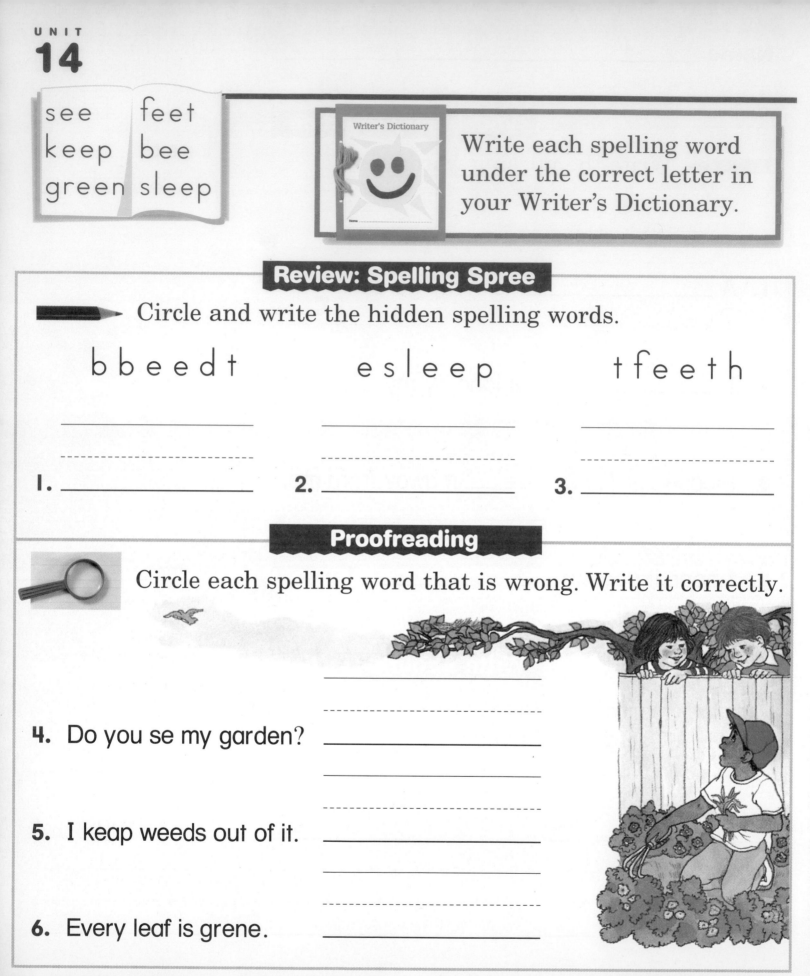

Skill: Children will find, circle, and write hidden spelling words. They will circle misspelled spelling words and will write them correctly.

Home Activity: Give your child a practice spelling test. Say each spelling word aloud, and use it in a sentence. Have your child write each spelling word.

Name _____

Special Words for Writing

| some | about | or |

HIGH-FREQUENCY WORDS

✏️ Write the Special Words.

1. some

2. about

3. or

_____

_____

_____

_____

_____

_____

✏️🖍️ Write the missing Special Words.
Color the picture.

_____

4. Dad knows a lot _____ gardens.

_____

5. He has _____ tall plants.

_____

6. Jim _____ I will help him.

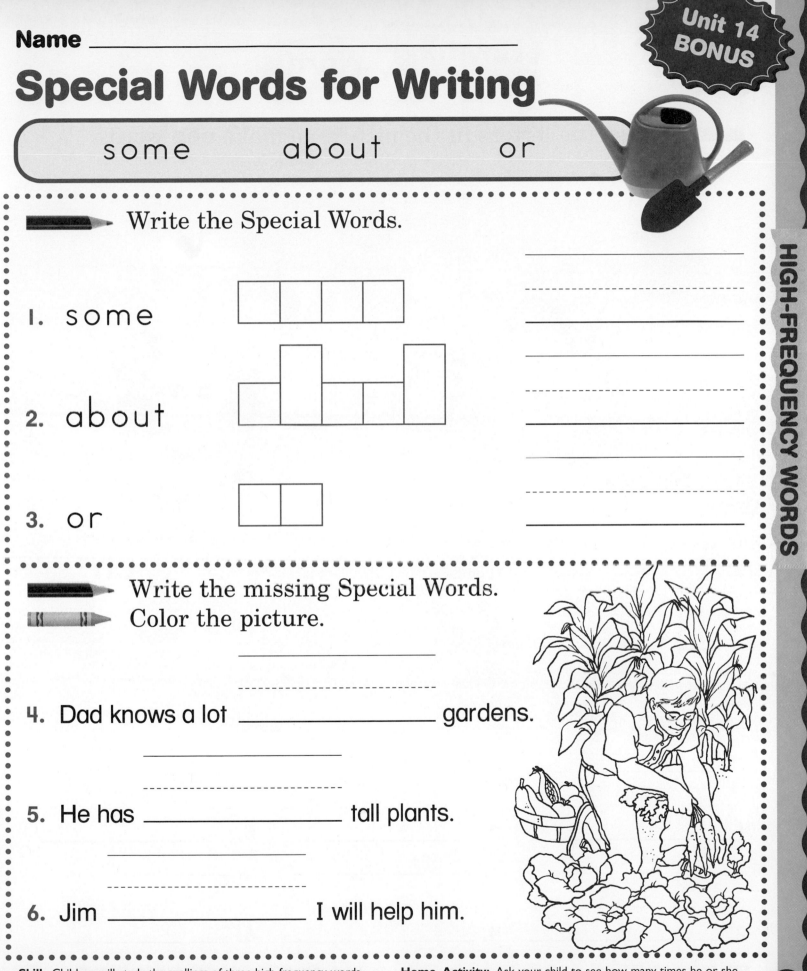

Skill: Children will study the spellings of three high-frequency words. They will write each word in configuration boxes, in isolation, and in a sentence.

Home Activity: Ask your child to see how many times he or she can find the three Special Words on a printed page from a magazine or newspaper article about gardening.

Rhyming Words

Use the letters in the picture to make **eep** words.

1. _____

2. _____

3. _____

4. _____

5. _____

6. _____

Skill: Children will build new words by adding letters to a phonogram learned in this unit.

Home Activity: Discuss the picture with your child. Share something you know about gardening, or together, read a book about this topic.

15 Review: Units 13–14

Unit 13 Words Spelled with c l, f l, or s l (pages 121–126)

clap	flag	flat
sled	club	slip

Finish the sentences. Write a word for each picture.

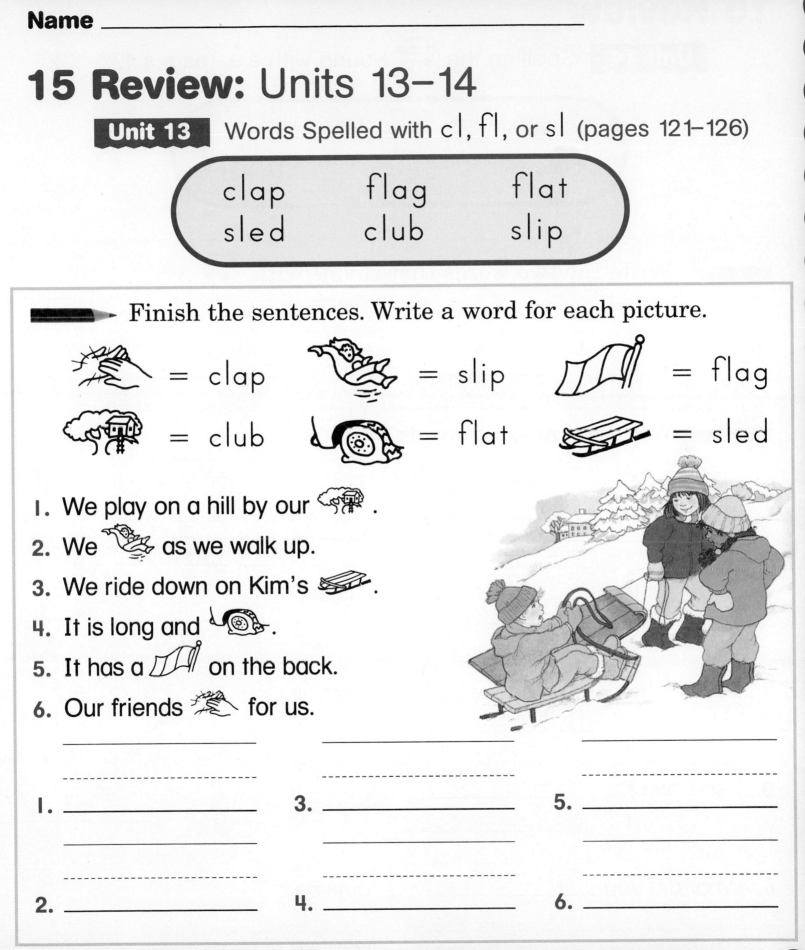

= clap   = slip   = flag

= club   = flat   = sled

1. We play on a hill by our 🏠 .

2. We 🐦 as we walk up.

3. We ride down on Kim's 🛷 .

4. It is long and 🐌 .

5. It has a 🚩 on the back.

6. Our friends 👏 for us.

1. _____

2. _____

3. _____

4. _____

5. _____

6. _____

Skill: Children will complete sentences by writing spelling words to match picture clues.

Home Activity: Pour some salt or sand into a small box or tin. Have your child write each spelling word in the salt or sand with a finger. Shake the box gently to erase each word.

133

15 Review

see	green	bee
keep	feet	sleep

Write the two words that rhyme with 🐑 .

_____   _____

- - - - - - - - - - - - - - -   - - - - - - - - - - - - - - -

1. _____   2. _____

Write the missing words.

_____

- - - - - - - - - - - - - - - - - - - -

3. I saw a little _____ outside.

_____

- - - - - - - - - - - - - - - - - - - -

4. I saw some _____ grass.

_____

- - - - - - - - - - - - - - - - - - - -

5. I saw two big _____ .

_____

- - - - - - - - - - - - - - - - - - - -

6. What did you _____ outside?

Skill: Children will write spelling words that rhyme with a picture name. They will write spelling words to complete sentences.

Home Activity: Print several simple sentences on a sheet of paper. Misspell one spelling word in each sentence. Ask your child to find and correct the words that you misspelled.

Good As New
by Barbara Douglass

1. Get Ready

Draw a picture of something nice you did with someone in your family.

Skill: Children will listen to and then discuss a personal narrative. They will complete a prewriting activity in which they explore a topic by drawing.

Home Activity: Have your child tell you about his or her drawing.

LITERATURE AND WRITING: A Story About Me

2. Write

Write a story about what you are doing in your picture.

Word Bank

us   we   make   keep   ★were   ★some

_____

_____

_____

_____

_____

_____

_____

_____

_____

_____

_____

_____

3. Write More

4. Proofread

5. Make a Final Copy

Skill: Children will write a first draft, revise, proofread, and publish a personal narrative.

Home Activity: Have your child read aloud his or her story. Share an interesting or funny experience you had with another member of the family.

Name _____

Words Spelled with st

LOOK ⟩ SAY ⟩ THINK ⟩ WRITE ⟩ CHECK

1. stop _____ _____

2. must _____ _____

3. just _____ _____

4. step _____ _____

5. best _____ _____

6. fast _____ _____

What is the sound of **st**?
Draw a line under **st** in each word you wrote.

Skill: Children will study the spellings of six words that begin or end with the consonant cluster **st**. They will write each word twice and will underline **st**.

Home Activity: Have your child read, spell aloud, and trace with a finger each numbered word. Say additional words. Ask your child to say "stop" after each word with **st**.

stop step
must best
just fast

Practice

Write the word that begins like each picture name.

1. _____

2. _____

3. _____

4. _____

Write the two words that begin like ☆.

5. _____

6. _____

Write the four words that end like 🏠.

7. _____

8. _____

9. _____

10. _____

Skill: Children will write spelling words that begin and end like picture names.

Home Activity: With your child, review the spelling of each word on the list. Together, make up some tongue twisters, using spelling words and other words spelled with **st**.

stop | step
must | best
just | fast

Vocabulary Practice

Write the missing words.

_____

1. We _____ onto the track.

2. We _____ run very _____.

3. I can _____ when the race ends.

4. The finish is _____ over there.

Write About a Race

Write a sentence about winning a race.
Use **best** in your sentence.

_____

_____

_____

_____

Skill: Children will write spelling words to complete sentences. They will write an original sentence, using one spelling word.

Home Activity: Ask your child to name his or her favorite outdoor game or sport. Have your child describe this game or sport, using some of the spelling words.

stop step
must best
just fast

Write each spelling word under the correct letter in your Writer's Dictionary.

Writer's Dictionary

Review: Spelling Spree

Write the spelling word for each clue.

1. It means **not slow**.

2. It means **do not go**.

3. Feet do this.

1. →

2. ↓

3. →

Proofreading

Circle each spelling word that is wrong. Write it correctly.

4. Tom jest jumped to me. _____

5. Now I muts jump to Ben. _____

6. I do my bist to go fast. _____

Skill: Children will complete a crossword puzzle by writing spelling words to match printed clues. They will circle misspelled spelling words and will write them correctly.

Home Activity: Give your child a practice spelling test. Say each spelling word aloud, and use it in a sentence. Have your child write each spelling word.

Special Words for Writing

their   other   your

HIGH-FREQUENCY WORDS

Write the Special Words.

1. their

2. other

3. your

_____

_____

_____

_____

_____

_____

Write the missing Special Words.

_____

4. You wear red hats on _____ team.

_____

5. They wear blue hats on _____ team.

_____

6. The _____ team wears green hats.

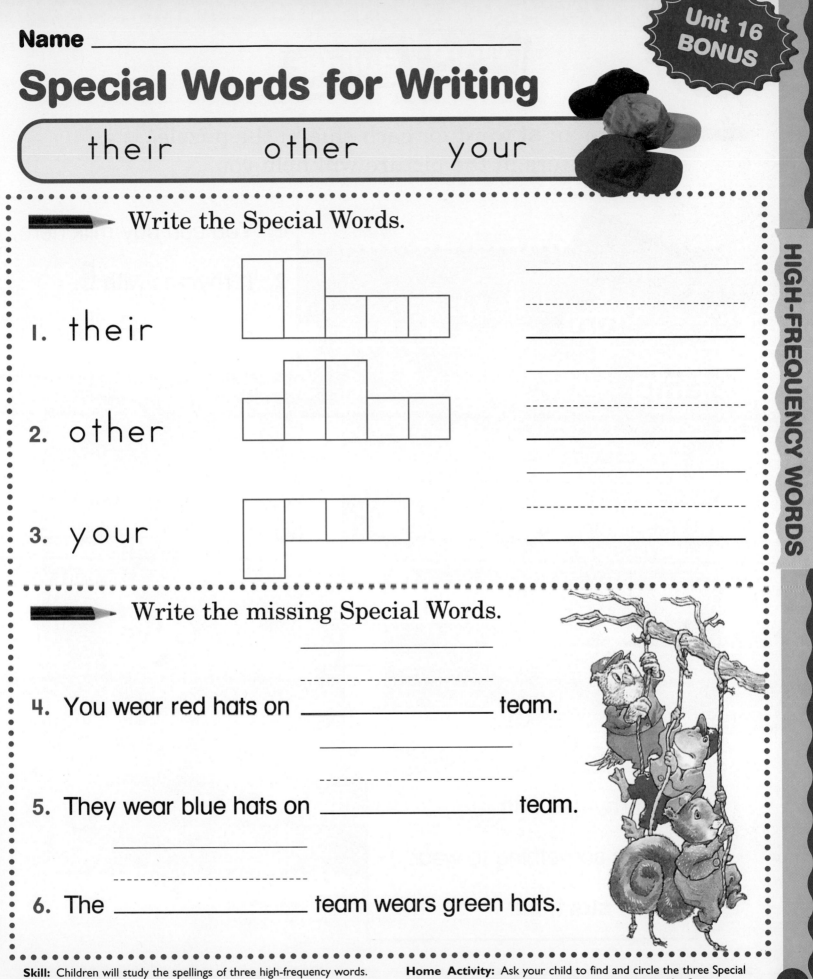

Skill: Children will study the spellings of three high-frequency words. They will write each word in configuration boxes, in isolation, and in a sentence.

Home Activity: Ask your child to find and circle the three Special Words on a printed page from a sports magazine or the Sports section of the newspaper.

Word Builder

Write an **st** word for each clue in the puzzle.
The letters in the picture will help you.

PHONICS AND SPELLING

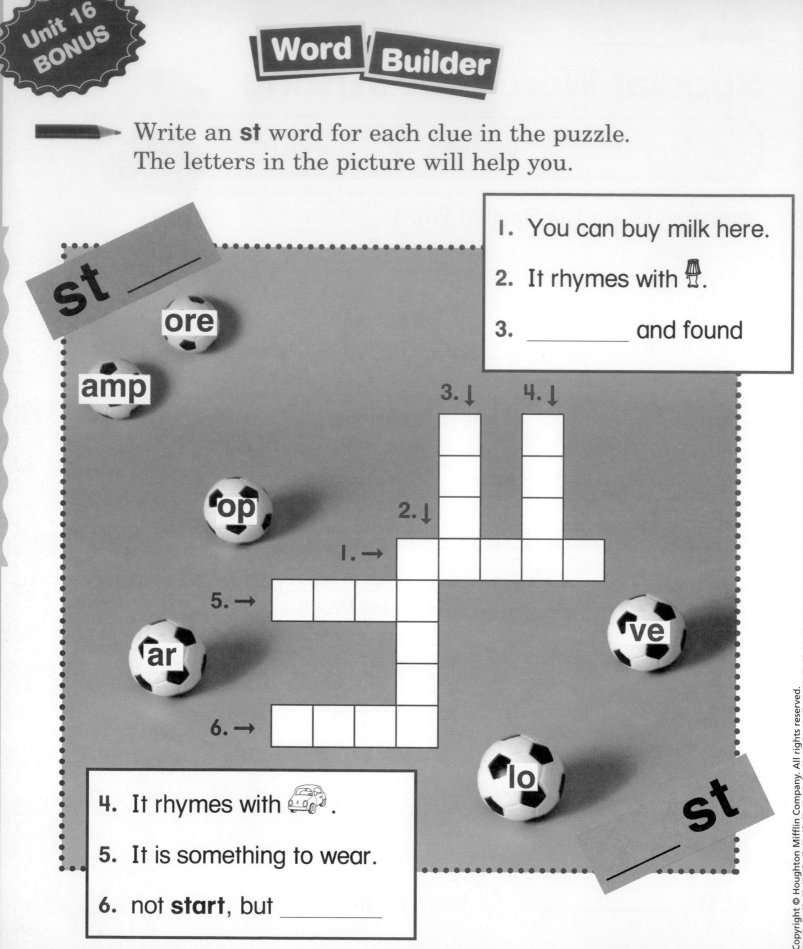

1. You can buy milk here.

2. It rhymes with 🪔.

3. _____ and found

4. It rhymes with 🚗.

5. It is something to wear.

6. not **start**, but _____

Skill: Children will build new words by adding **st** to other word parts.

Home Activity: Discuss the picture with your child. Share something you know about field sports, or together, read a book about this topic.

Spelling the  Sound with ay

LOOK SAY THINK WRITE CHECK

1. day
2. say
3. play
4. may
5. way
6. stay

What two letters spell the  sound?
Draw a line under these letters in each word you wrote.

Skill: Children will study the spellings of six words with the |ā| sound. They will write each word twice and will underline the letters that spell the |ā| sound. **Picture clue: apron**

Home Activity: Have your child read, spell aloud, and trace with a finger each numbered word. Together, say the names of days of the week and holidays that have the **apron** sound spelled **ay**.

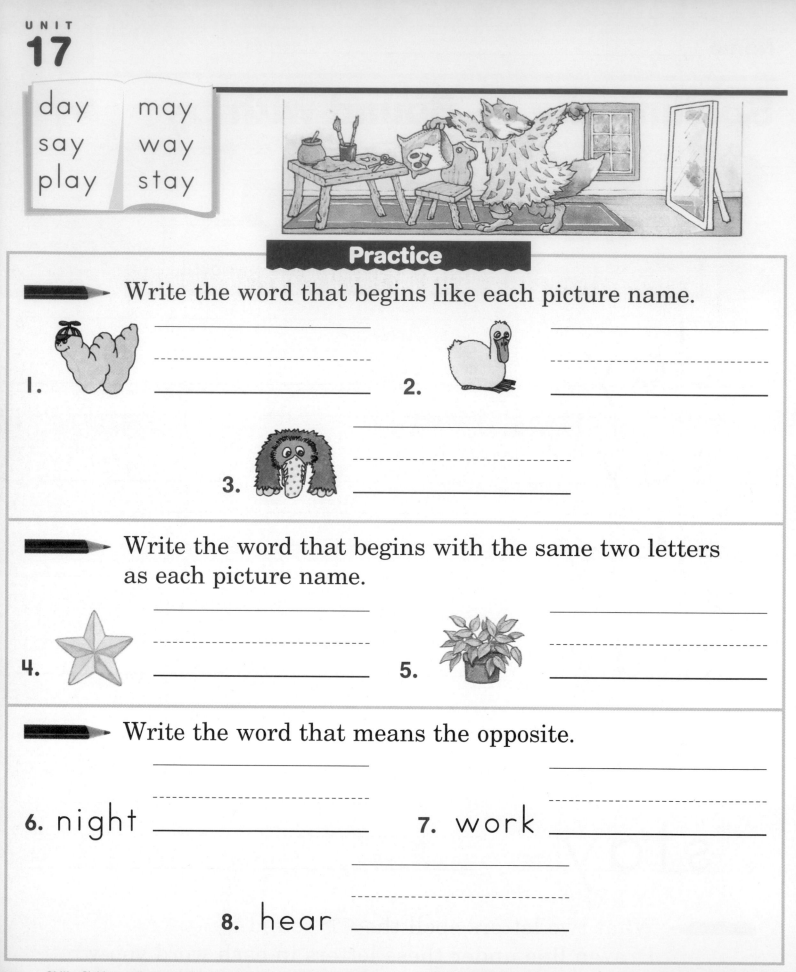

day   may
say   way
play   stay

Practice

➤ Write the word that begins like each picture name.

1. _____

2. _____

3. _____

➤ Write the word that begins with the same two letters as each picture name.

4. _____

5. _____

➤ Write the word that means the opposite.

6. night _____

7. work _____

8. hear _____

Skill: Children will write spelling words that begin like picture names. They will write spelling words with the opposite meanings of printed word clues.

Home Activity: With your child, review the spelling of each word on the list. Together, make a list of other words that rhyme with the spelling words and that end with **ay**.

day	may
say	way
play	stay

Vocabulary Practice

➤ Write the missing words.

_____

1. My class is in a _____ .

2. I will _____ late to _____ my part.

3. My dad likes the _____ I act.

4. We _____ put our show on soon.

Write About a Play

Write a sentence about a play you have seen.
Use **day** in your sentence.

_____

_____

_____

_____

Skill: Children will write spelling words to complete sentences. They will write an original sentence, using one spelling word.

Home Activity: Ask your child to pretend that he or she has written a play. Ask your child to tell about the play, using some of the spelling words.

day   may
say   way
play stay

Writer's Dictionary

Name _____

Write each spelling word under the correct letter in your Writer's Dictionary.

Review: Spelling Spree

Write the letter for each shape. Make spelling words.

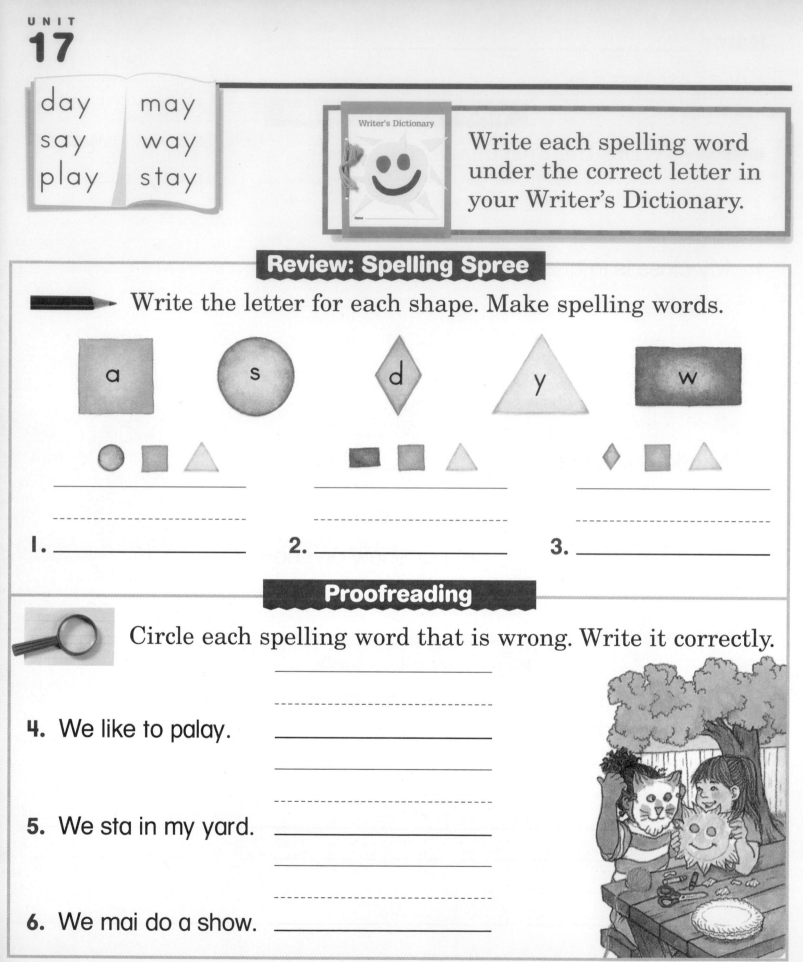

a   s   d   y   w

1. _____

2. _____

3. _____

Proofreading

Circle each spelling word that is wrong. Write it correctly.

_____

4. We like to palay.   _____

_____

5. We sta in my yard.   _____

_____

6. We mai do a show.   _____

Skill: Children will use a code to write spelling words. They will circle misspelled spelling words and will write them correctly.

Home Activity: Give your child a practice spelling test. Say each spelling word aloud, and use it in a sentence. Have your child write each spelling word.

Special Words for Writing

could   has   very

✏️ Write the Special Words.

1. could

2. has

3. very

_____

_____

_____

_____

_____

_____

✏️ Write the missing Special Words.

4. Fox _____ a part in the play.

5. He sings _____ well.

6. Fox _____ be a star!

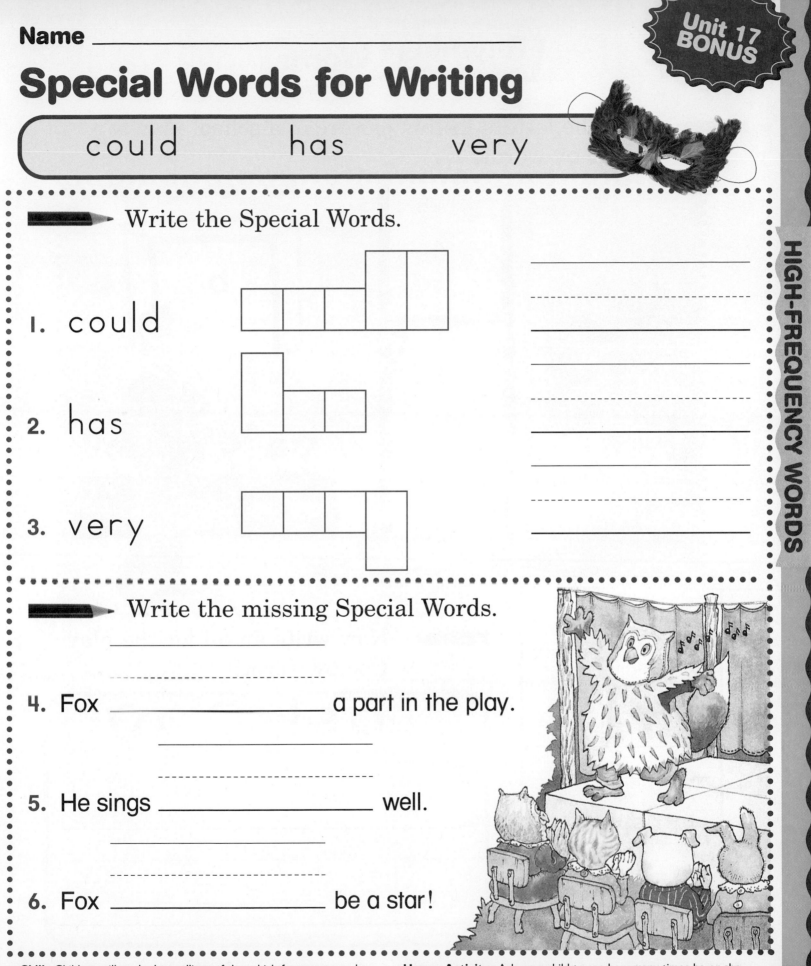

Skill: Children will study the spellings of three high-frequency words. They will write each word in configuration boxes, in isolation, and in a sentence.

Home Activity: Ask your child to see how many times he or she can find the three Special Words on a printed page from the Entertainment section of the newspaper.

Rhyming Words

Use the letters in this picture of a school play to make **ay** words.

1. _____

2. _____

3. _____

4. _____

Now write an ad for the play.
Use **ay** words.

Lost Dog

5. _____

Skill: Children will build new words by adding letters to a phonogram learned in this unit. They will write sentences, using words with the **ay** phonogram.

Home Activity: Discuss the picture with your child. Share something you know about the theater, or together, read a book about this topic.

18 Review: Units 16–17

Unit 16 Words Spelled with st (pages 137–142)

stop	just	best
must	step	fast

Write the two words that have the ☂ sound.

_____   _____

1. _____   2. _____

Write the missing words.
Color the picture.

_____

3. This race is the _____ of all.

_____

4. Take one _____ at a time.

_____

5. Do not move too _____.

_____

6. Please _____ at the white line.

Skill: Children will write spelling words that have the |ŭ| sound. They will write spelling words to complete sentences.

Home Activity: Have your child give you a test on the spelling words. Print each word as your child reads it to you. Ask your child to correct your spelling test.

18 Review

 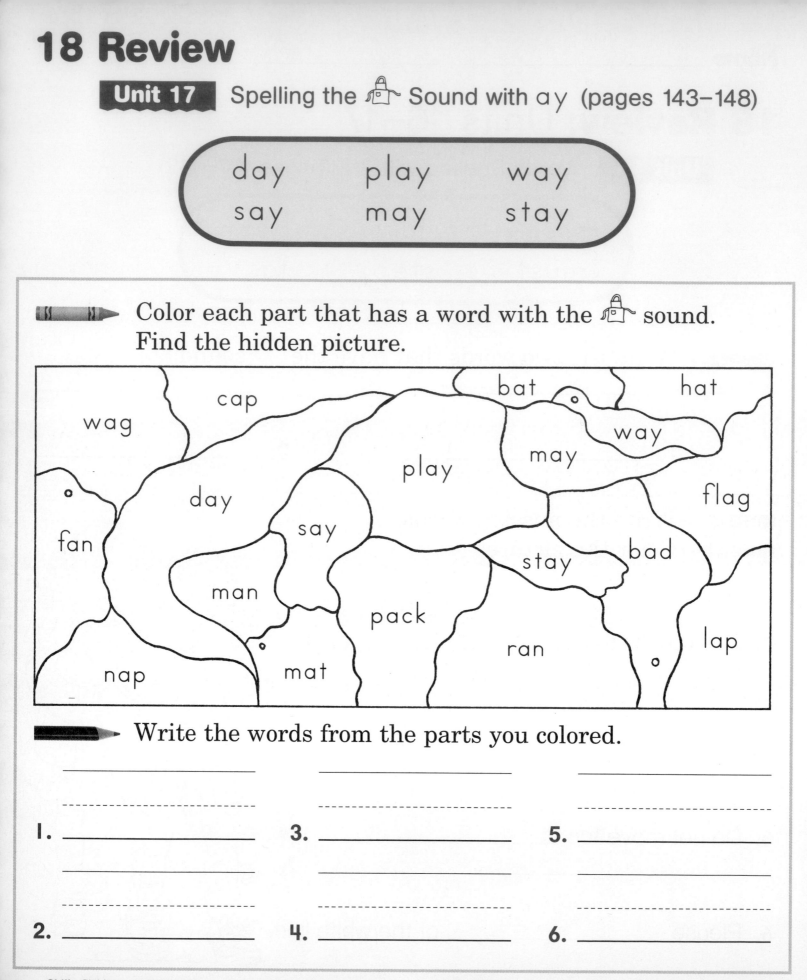

day	play	way
say	may	stay

Color each part that has a word with the 👜 sound.
Find the hidden picture.

wag cap bat hat

way

may

play

day

flag

say

fan

stay bad

man

pack

ran lap

nap mat

Write the words from the parts you colored.

1. _____   3. _____   5. _____

2. _____   4. _____   6. _____

Skill: Children will find a hidden picture by coloring shapes containing spelling words with the |ā| sound. They will write each spelling word.

Home Activity: Print each spelling word on a piece of heavy paper. Cut each word into three or four puzzle pieces. Have your child put the pieces together to make the spelling words.

150

We Are Best Friends
by Aliki

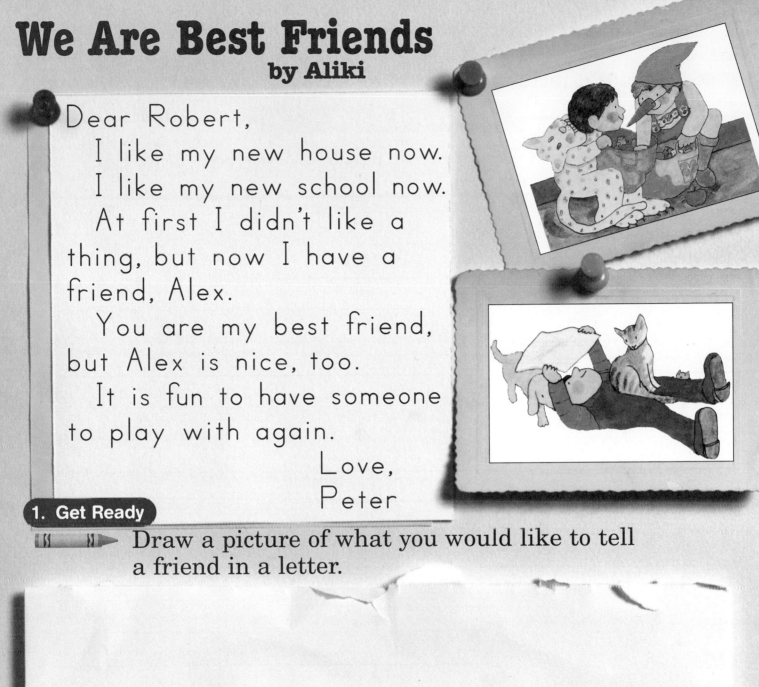

Dear Robert,
   I like my new house now.
I like my new school now.
   At first I didn't like a
thing, but now I have a
friend, Alex.
   You are my best friend,
but Alex is nice, too.
   It is fun to have someone
to play with again.
                    Love,
                    Peter

1. Get Ready

Draw a picture of what you would like to tell
a friend in a letter.

LITERATURE AND WRITING: A Letter

Skill: Children will listen to and then discuss a story and a letter
excerpted from it. They will complete a prewriting activity in which
they explore a topic by drawing.

Home Activity: Have your child tell you about his or her drawing.

UNIT

18 The Writing Process

LITERATURE AND WRITING: A Letter

2. Write

Write a letter to your friend.

Word Bank

fun me best may ★ said ★ your

___________________,

____

____

____

___________________,

____

3. Write More

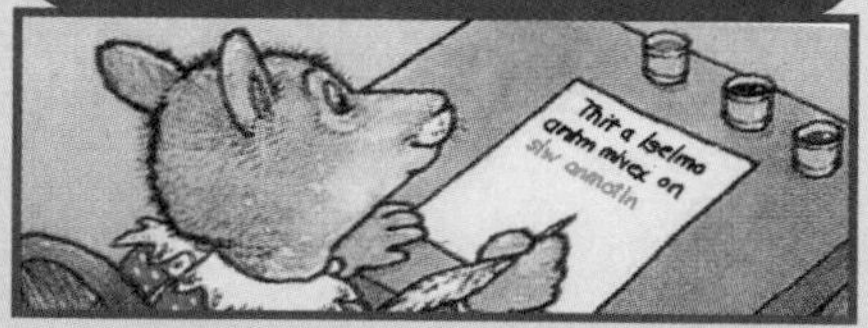

4. Proofread

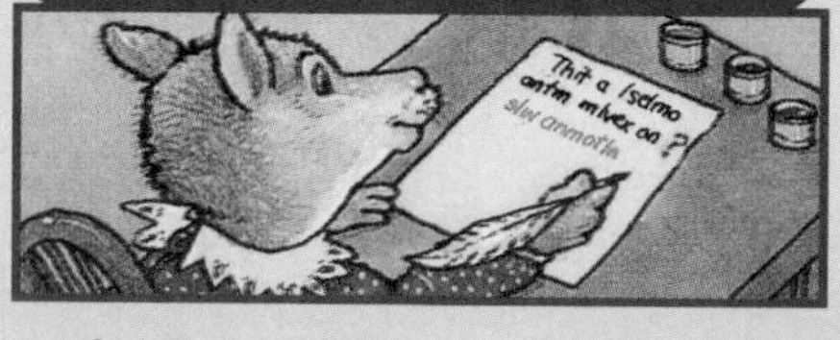

5. Make a Final Copy

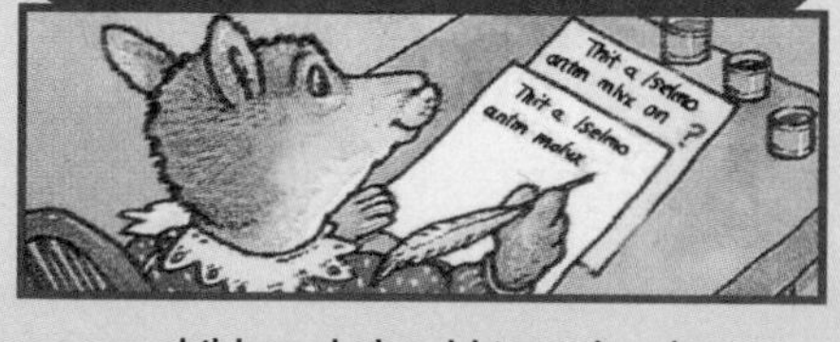

Skill: Children will write a first draft, revise, proofread, and publish a letter.

Home Activity: Have your child read aloud his or her letter. Together, address an envelope, and mail the letter your child has written.

Name _____

Words Spelled with sh **or** ch

1. she

2. chin

3. fish

4. shop

5. much

6. chop

What are the sounds of **sh** and **ch**?
Draw a line under **sh** or **ch** in each word you wrote.

Skill: Children will study the spellings of six words with the |sh| or the |ch| sound. They will write each word twice and will underline **sh** or **ch**.

Home Activity: Have your child read, spell aloud, and trace with a finger each numbered word. Say each spelling word. Ask your child to say "cheese" after each word with **ch**.

153

she   shop
chin   much
fish   chop

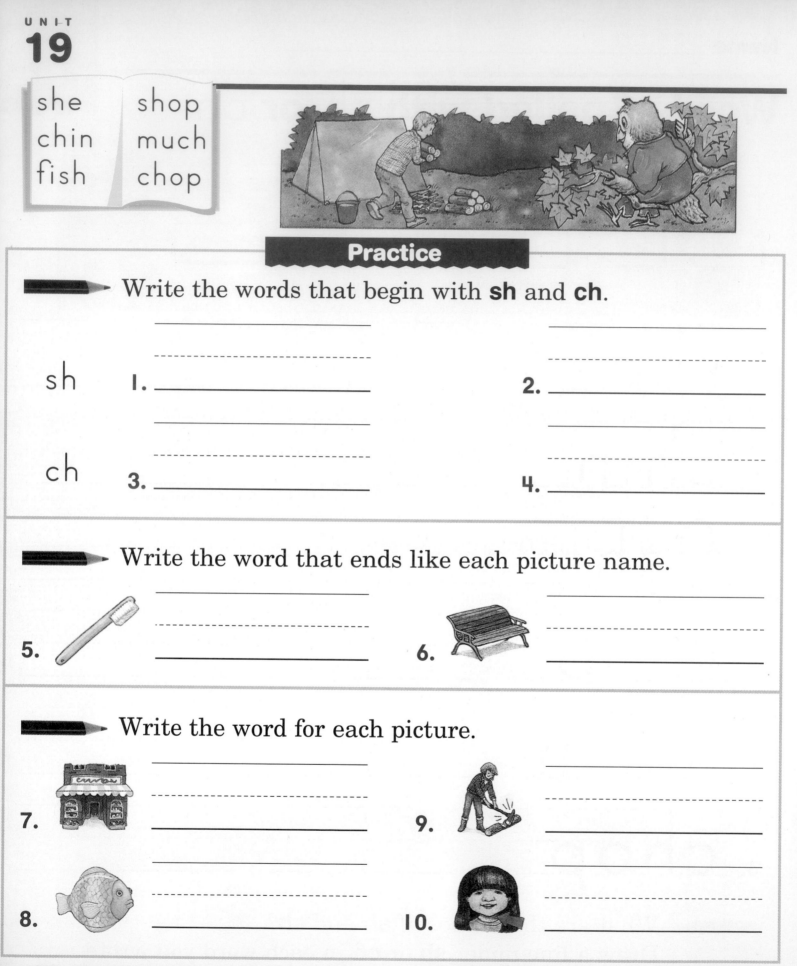

Practice

Write the words that begin with **sh** and **ch**.

sh   1. _____   2. _____

ch   3. _____   4. _____

Write the word that ends like each picture name.

5. _____   6. _____

Write the word for each picture.

7. _____   9. _____

8. _____   10. _____

Skill: Children will write spelling words that begin or end with **sh** or **ch**. They will write spelling words that name pictures.

Home Activity: With your child, review the spelling of each word on the list. Say "She sells seashells by the seashore." Together make up other tongue twisters, using **ch** words.

Name _____

Vocabulary Practice

she	shop
chin	much
fish	chop

✏️ Write the missing words.
🖍️ Color the picture.

_____

1. We have so _____ to do!

2. Frog and I _____ wood.

3. Bits of wood hit his _____ .

4. I catch _____ in the lake.

Write About Camping

📓 Write a sentence about getting ready to go camping. Use **she** and **shop** in your sentence.

_____

_____

_____

_____

Skill: Children will write spelling words to complete sentences. They will write an original sentence, using two spelling words.

Home Activity: Have your child pretend that he or she has chosen the best spot in the forest to camp. Ask your child to use some of the spelling words to tell why he or she chose this spot.

she   shop
chin   much
fish   chop

Writer's Dictionary

Name _____

Write each spelling word under the correct letter in your Writer's Dictionary.

Review: Spelling Spree

Circle and write the hidden spelling words.

xshopl   dmbshe   chopik

_____   _____   _____

- - - - - - -   - - - - - - -   - - - - - - -

1. _____   2. _____   3. _____

Proofreading

Circle each spelling word that is wrong. Write it correctly.

_____

- - - - - - - - - - - -

4. There is too moch rain!   _____

_____

- - - - - - - - - - - -

5. Even my chen is wet.   _____

_____

- - - - - - - - - - - -

6. I wish I were a fich.   _____

Skill: Children will find, circle, and write hidden spelling words. They will circle misspelled spelling words and will write them correctly.

Home Activity: Give your child a practice spelling test. Say each spelling word aloud, and use it in a sentence. Have your child write each spelling word.

Special Words for Writing

now	look	our

HIGH-FREQUENCY WORDS

Write the Special Words.

1. now

2. look

3. our

_____

Write the missing Special Words.

4. Come _____ at this stove.

5. We can cook dinner _____ .

6. We will eat in _____ tent.

Skill: Children will study the spellings of three high-frequency words. They will write each word in configuration boxes, in isolation, and in a sentence.

Home Activity: Ask your child to find the three Special Words in a catalog or a circular. Have your child cut out the words and paste them on this page.

Word Builder

Write **sh** to finish each word. Then write the word.

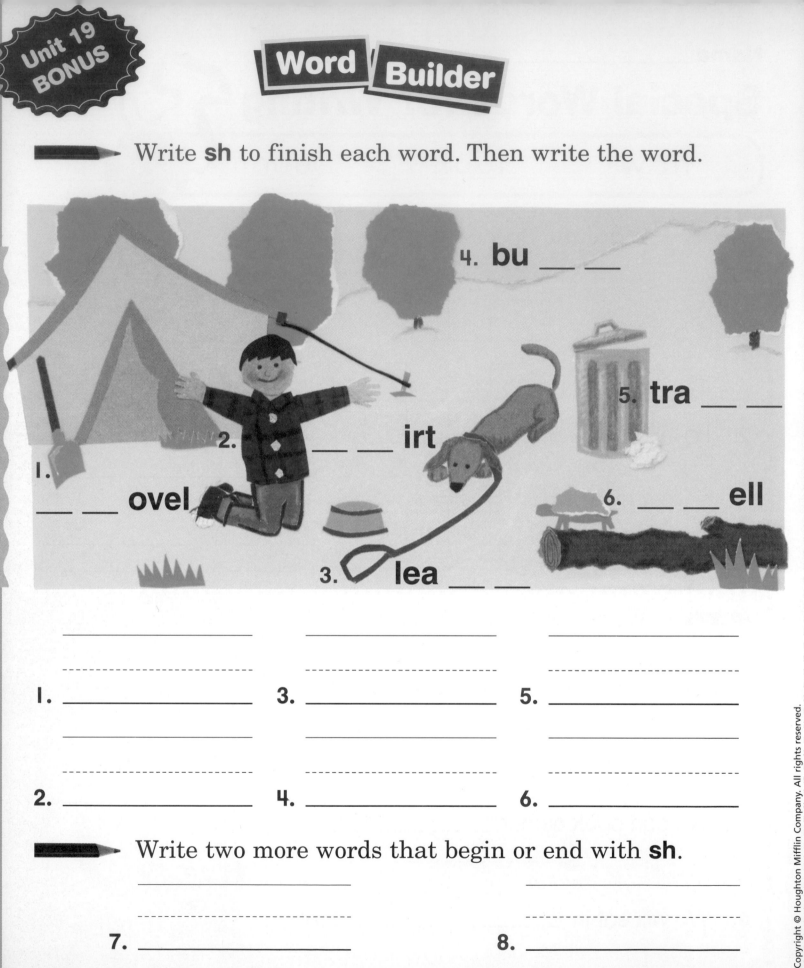

4. bu __ __

5. tra __ __

2. __ __ irt

1. __ __ ovel

6. __ __ ell

3. lea __ __

1. _____

2. _____

3. _____

4. _____

5. _____

6. _____

Write two more words that begin or end with **sh**.

7. _____

8. _____

Skill: Children will build new words by adding **sh** to other word parts.

Home Activity: Discuss the picture with your child. Share something you know about camping, or together, read a book about this topic.

Adding s to Naming Words

| LOOK | SAY | THINK | WRITE | CHECK |

1. cup _____ _____

2. cups _____ _____

3. frog _____ _____

4. frogs _____ _____

5. kite _____ _____

6. kites _____ _____

What letter makes some words mean more than one?
Draw a line under this letter in the words you wrote.

Skill: Children will study the spellings of three nouns in their singular and plural forms. They will write each word twice and will underline the **s** in each plural noun.

Home Activity: Have your child read, spell aloud, and trace each numbered word. Together, finish these sentences, using words that add **s** to name more than one. **I see one ___. I see some ___.**

cup	frogs
cups	kite
frog	kites

Practice

Write the two words with the 🧊 sound.

1. _____

2. _____

Write the two words with the ☂ sound.

3. _____

4. _____

Write the word for each picture.

5. _____

6. _____

7. _____

8. _____

9. _____

10. _____

Skill: Children will write spelling words with the |ī| and the |ŭ| sounds. They will write spelling words that name pictures.

Home Activity: With your child, review the spelling of each word on the list. Say these words from earlier units: **cat**, **game**, and **flag**. Have your child add **s** to write three new words.

cup	frogs
cups	kite
frog	kites

Vocabulary Practice

✏️ Write the missing words.

_____

_____

1. I drink from a _____ .

_____

_____

2. We watch two _____ fly.

_____

_____

3. Some _____ watch us.

_____

_____

4. One _____ jumps into Ana's lap!

Write About a Picnic

✏️ Write a sentence about what to bring on a picnic.
Use **kite** and **cups** in your sentence.

_____

_____

_____

_____

Skill: Children will write spelling words to complete sentences. They will write an original sentence, using two spelling words.

Home Activity: Have your child pretend that he or she is one of the frogs in the story above. Ask your child to describe the picnic scene, using some of the spelling words.

cup frogs
cups kite
frog kites

Writer's Dictionary

Name _____

Write each spelling word under the correct letter in your Writer's Dictionary.

Review: Spelling Spree

Add and take away letters. Write the spelling words.

1. cubs – b + p = ?

2. k + bites – b = ?

3. fr + hogs – h = ?

_____ _____ _____

1. _____ 2. _____ 3. _____

Proofreading

Circle each spelling word that is wrong. Write it correctly.

_____

4. I like to fly my cite. _____

5. It is green like a frug. _____

6. My kup is green too. _____

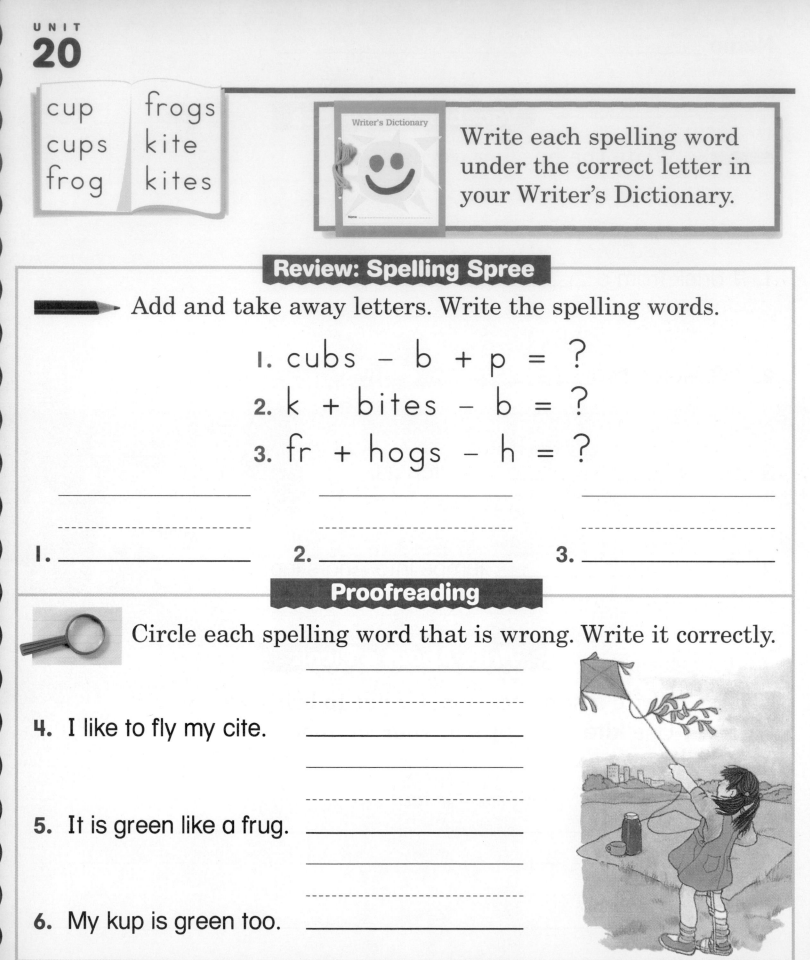

Skill: Children will add and subtract letters to write spelling words. They will circle misspelled spelling words and will write them correctly.

Home Activity: Give your child a practice spelling test. Say each spelling word aloud, and use it in a sentence. Have your child write each spelling word.

Special Words for Writing

into   over   two

Write the Special Words.

1. into

2. over

3. two

_____
_____
_____
_____
_____
_____
_____

Write the missing Special Words.
Color the picture.

_____

4. The picnic was _____ .

5. Frog left with _____ pals.

6. They jumped _____ the pond.

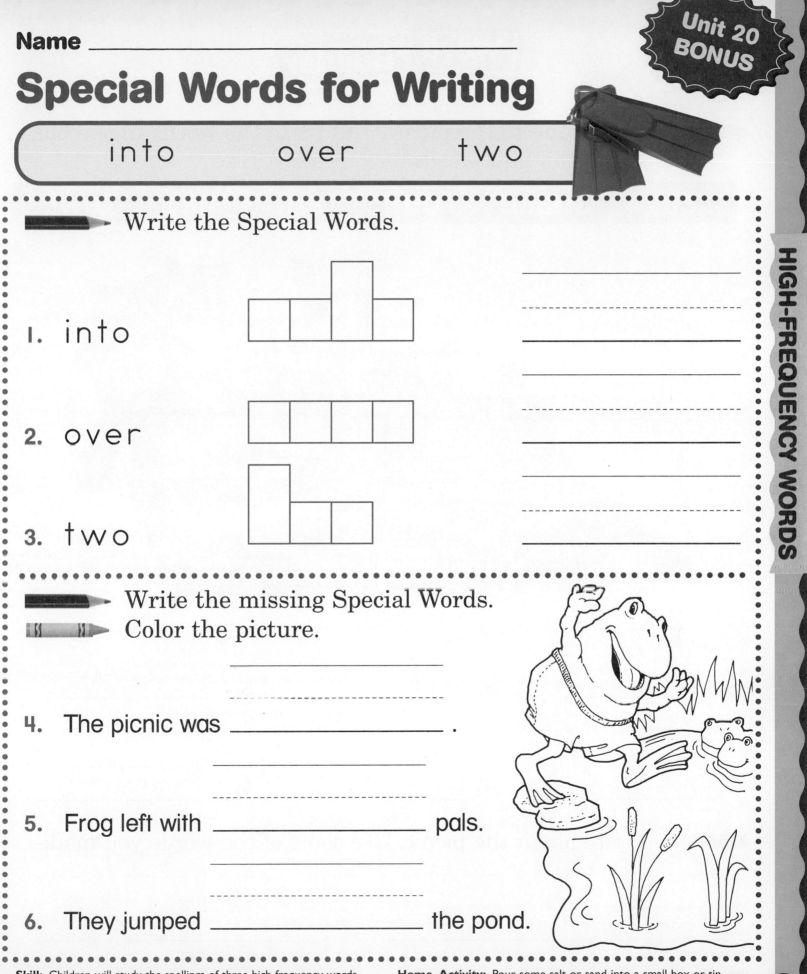

Skill: Children will study the spellings of three high-frequency words. They will write each word in configuration boxes, in isolation, and in a sentence.

Home Activity: Pour some salt or sand into a small box or tin. Have your child write each Special Word in the salt or the sand with a finger. Shake the box gently to erase each word.

Who came to the picnic? Add **s** to the words in the box. Write the new words.

cat	snake	dog	ant	bee	owl

1. _____

2. _____

3. _____

4. _____

5. _____

6. _____

Write about the picnic. Use some of the words you made.

_____

_____

_____

Skill: Children will build new words by adding **s** to singular nouns. They will write a sentence using one of the words they made.

Home Activity: Discuss the picture with your child. Share something you know about picnicking, or together, read a book about this topic.

21 Review: Units 19–20

Unit 19   Words Spelled with sh or ch (pages 153–158)

> she   fish   much
>
> chin   shop   chop

Write the two words that rhyme with ✎ .

_____   _____

1. _____   2. _____

Write the missing words.
Color the picture.

_____

3. Pam just got a new _____ .

_____

4. I know that _____ likes it.

_____

5. It can do so _____ .

_____

6. It jumps as high as Pam's _____ !

Skill: Children will write spelling words that rhyme with a picture name. They will write spelling words to complete sentences.

Home Activity: Provide your child with toothpicks, straws, or cotton swabs. Say each spelling word. Have your child form the letters in each word, using the chosen material.

21 Review

Unit 20 Adding s to Naming Words (pages 159–164)

cup	frog	kite
cups	frogs	kites

Finish the sentences. Write words for the shapes.

◯ = cup   △ = frog   ◇ = kite

◯◯ = cups   △△△ = frogs   ◇◇ = kites

1. We take our ◇◇ to the park.

2. My ◇ has a star on it.

3. Small △△△ live in the park.

4. One △ has spots on its back.

5. Jim gets ◯◯ of water for us.

6. I throw my ◯ in the can.

1. _____

2. _____

3. _____

4. _____

5. _____

6. _____

Skill: Children will complete sentences by writing spelling words to match shapes.

Home Activity: Have your child cut the letters **c, e, f, g, i, k, o, p, r, s, t,** and **u** from newspaper or magazine headlines. Have your child use the letters to spell each word.

Copyright © Houghton Mifflin Company. All rights reserved.

CLYDE MONSTER

by Robert L. Crowe

Clyde wasn't very big, but he was ugly. And he was getting uglier every day. He lived in the woods with his mother and father.

Father Monster was a big monster. He was very ugly, which was good. Mother Monster was even uglier, which was better. Monsters laugh at pretty monsters. All in all, Clyde and his mother and father were lovely monsters — as monsters go.

All day Clyde played in the woods doing lovely monster things. He liked to make big holes, and he liked to walk into things. At night Clyde lived in a cave. But then one night he would not go into his cave.

"Why?" asked his mother. "Why won't you go into your cave?"

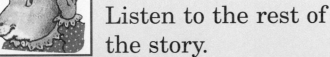 Listen to the rest of the story.

Skill: Children will listen to and discuss a fictional story.

Home Activity: Have your child tell you about the story **Clyde Monster**.

LITERATURE AND WRITING: A Story

1. Get Ready

Pretend you know a monster.
Draw a picture of the monster.

2. Write

Write a story about the monster and what it is afraid of.
Use another piece of paper.

Word Bank

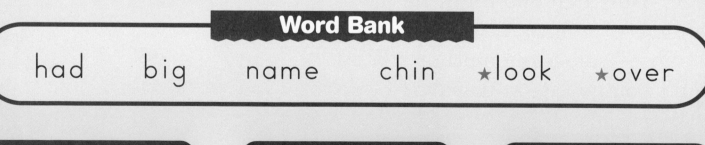

had   big   name   chin   ★look   ★over

3. Write More

4. Proofread

5. Make a Final Copy

Skill: Children will complete a prewriting activity in which they explore a topic by drawing. They will write a first draft, revise, proofread, and publish a fictional story.

Home Activity: Have your child read aloud his or her story. Together, talk about the story and the picture that goes with it.

Words Spelled with th or wh

LOOK SAY THINK WRITE CHECK

1. this _____ _____

2. when _____ _____

3. that _____ _____

4. with _____ _____

5. white _____ _____

6. bath _____ _____

What are the sounds of **th** and **wh**?
Draw a line under **th** or **wh** in each word you wrote.

Skill: Children will study the spellings of six words with the |th|, the
|th|, or the |hw| sound. They will write each word twice and will
underline **th** or **wh**.

Home Activity: Have your child read, spell aloud, and trace with a
finger each numbered word. Say the words **this, when, white,** and
bath. Ask your child to tell if each word has the **th** or the **wh** sound.

this	with
when	white
that	bath

Practice

Write the words that begin with **th** and **wh**.

th

1. _____   2. _____

wh

3. _____   4. _____

Write the two words that end with **th**.

5. _____   6. _____

Write the words with the 🏠 and the 🍎 sounds.

7. _____   8. _____

9. _____   10. _____

Skill: Children will write spelling words that begin with **th** and **wh** and that end with **th**. They will write spelling words with the |ĭ| and the |ă| sounds.

Home Activity: With your child, review the spelling of each word on the list. Together, make a list of other words that begin with **th** and **wh**.

this | with
when | white
that | bath

Vocabulary Practice

✏️ Write the missing words.

_____
- - - - - - - - - - - - - - - - - - -

1. I like the color _____ .

_____
- - - - - - - - - - - - - - - - - - -

2. I used it in _____ picture here.

_____
- - - - - - - - - - - - - - - - - - -

3. I cleaned up _____ I was done.

_____
- - - - - - - - - - - - - - - - - - -

4. Then I took a hot _____ .

Write About a Picture

📖 Write a sentence about a picture you painted.
Use **that** and **with** in your sentence.

_____
- -

_____
- -

_____

Skill: Children will write spelling words to complete sentences. They will write an original sentence, using two spelling words.

Home Activity: Ask your child to describe a painting or a picture in your home, using some of the spelling words.

this with
when white
that bath

Writer's Dictionary

Write each spelling word under the correct letter in your Writer's Dictionary.

Review: Spelling Spree

Write the spelling word for each clue.

1. This is the color of snow.
2. This will make you clean.
3. It is not this one, but _____ one.

1. _____
2. _____
3. _____

Proofreading

Circle each spelling word that is wrong. Write it correctly.

4. I painted thes picture. _____

5. I made it wen I was five. _____

6. I did it wit water colors. _____

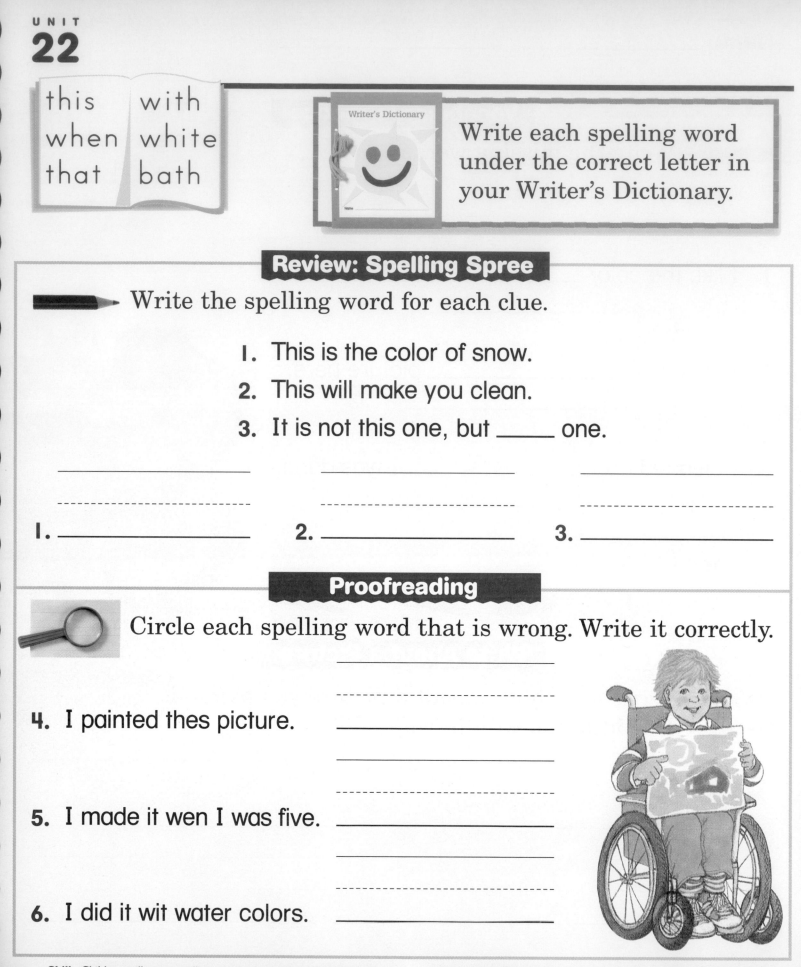

Skill: Children will write spelling words to match printed clues. They will circle misspelled spelling words and will write them correctly.

Home Activity: Give your child a practice spelling test. Say each spelling word aloud, and use it in a sentence. Have your child write each spelling word.

Special Words for Writing

| down | how | back |

Write the Special Words.

1. down

2. how

3. back

_____

Write the missing Special Words.
Color the picture.

_____

4. I know _____ to paint.

5. I paint a dog sitting _____ .

6. I put spots on its _____ .

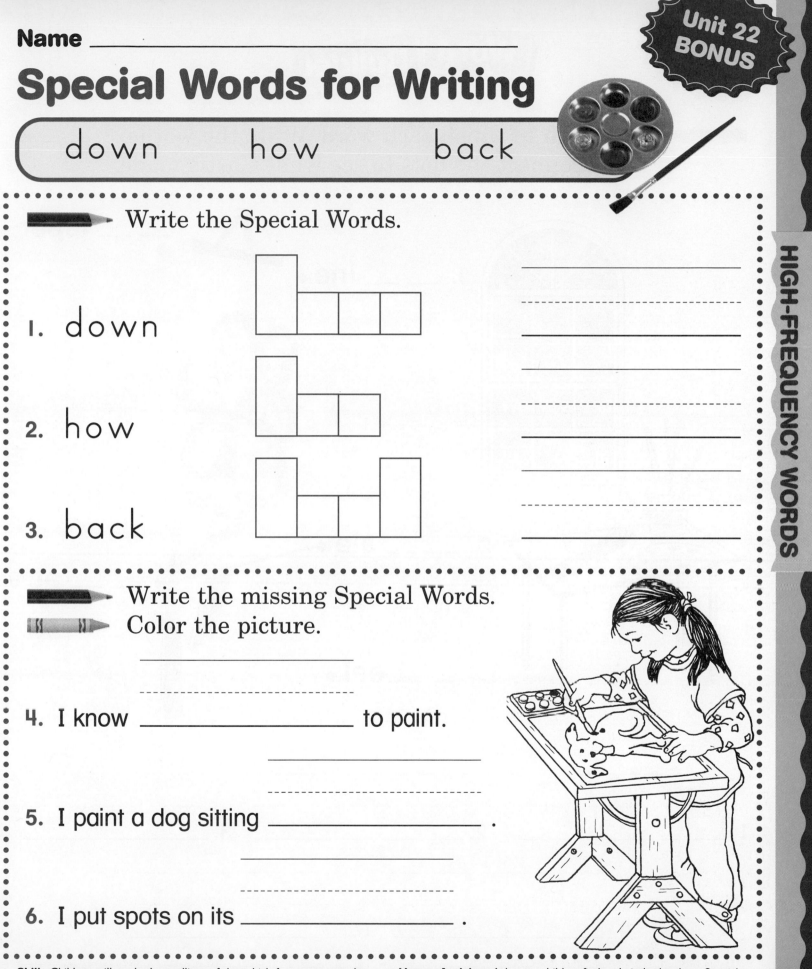

Skill: Children will study the spellings of three high-frequency words. They will write each word in configuration boxes, in isolation, and in a sentence.

Home Activity: Ask your child to find and circle the three Special Words on a printed page from a newspaper or a magazine.

173

Word Builder

Write **wh** to finish each word. Write the words.
Then connect the dots to see what Curtis made.

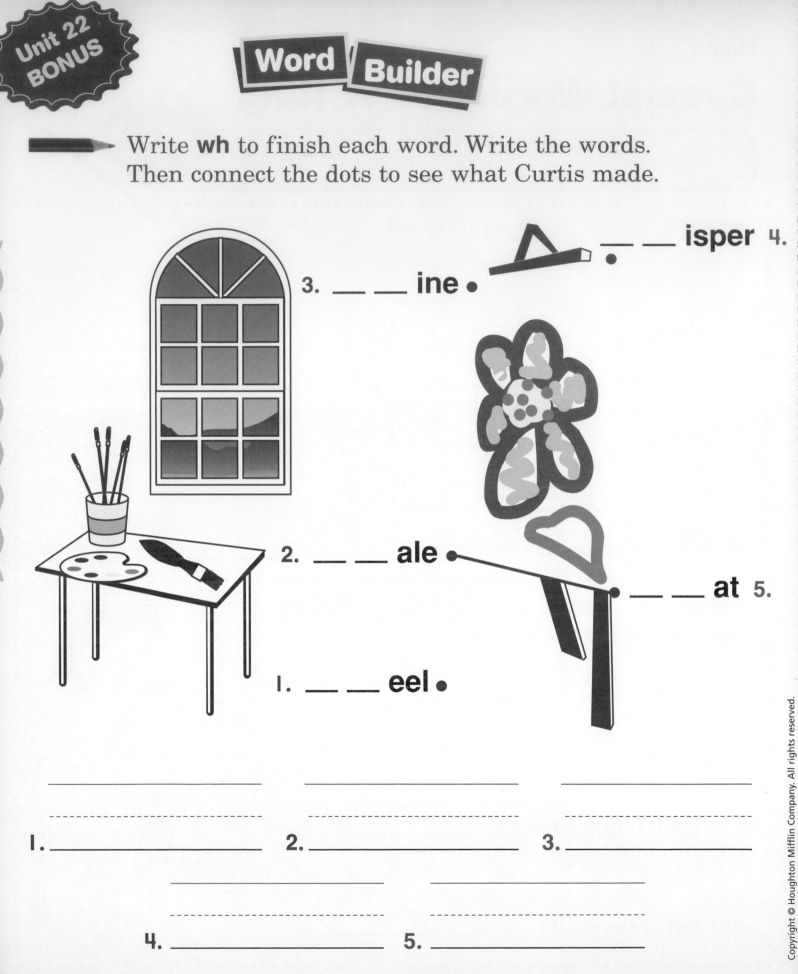

4. __ __ isper •

3. __ __ ine •

2. __ __ ale •

at 5.

1. __ __ eel •

_____   _____   _____

1. _____   2. _____   3. _____

_____   _____

4. _____   5. _____

Skill: Children will build new words by adding **wh** to word parts. They will write the words they made.

Home Activity: Discuss the picture with your child. Share something you know about painting, or together, read a book about this topic.

Spelling the  Sound with y

Name _____

LOOK ▸ SAY ▸ THINK ▸ WRITE ▸ CHECK

1. by

2. my

3. fly

4. sky

5. cry

6. why

What letter spells the ▨ sound?
Draw a line under this letter in each word you wrote.

Skill: Children will study the spellings of six words with the |ī| sound. They will write each word twice and will underline each letter that spells the |ī| sound. **Picture clue: ice**

Home Activity: Have your child read, spell aloud, and trace with a finger each numbered word. Say the words **me**, **try**, **hay**, and **spy**. Ask your child to name the words that end like **by**.

175

by	sky
my	cry
fly	why

Practice

Write the word that begins like each picture name.

1.

2.

Write the words that begin with the same sounds as the picture names.

3.

4.

5.

6.

Write the word for each picture.

7.

8.

9.

Skill: Children will write spelling words that begin like picture names. They will write spelling words that name pictures.

Home Activity: With your child, review the spelling of each word on the list. Together, make a list of other words that end with the **ice** sound spelled **y**. Examples: *try, shy, spy, dry*

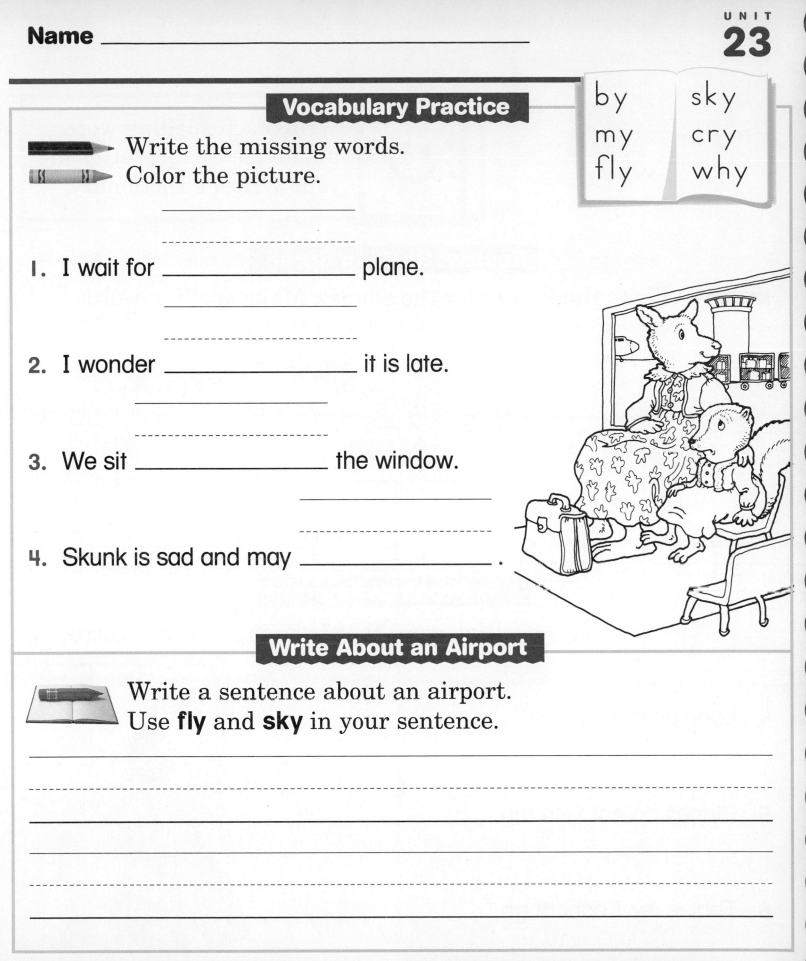

Vocabulary Practice

by   sky
my   cry
fly   why

Write the missing words.
Color the picture.

_____

- - - - - - - - - - - - - - - - - - -

1. I wait for _____ plane.

_____

- - - - - - - - - - - - - - - - - - -

2. I wonder _____ it is late.

_____

- - - - - - - - - - - - - - - - - - -

3. We sit _____ the window.

_____

- - - - - - - - - - - - - - - - - - -

4. Skunk is sad and may _____ .

Write About an Airport

Write a sentence about an airport.
Use **fly** and **sky** in your sentence.

_____

- - - - - - - - - - - - - - - - - - -

_____

- - - - - - - - - - - - - - - - - - -

_____

Skill: Children will write spelling words to complete sentences. They will write an original sentence, using two spelling words.

Home Activity: Ask your child to imagine that he or she is an airplane pilot. Have your child describe a flight, using some of the spelling words.

by   sky
my   cry
fly   why

Write each spelling word under the correct letter in your Writer's Dictionary.

Review: Spelling Spree

Write the letters for the shapes. Make spelling words.

y

b

m

cr

1. _____

2. _____

3. _____

Proofreading

Circle each spelling word that is wrong. Write it correctly.

4. Look up at the skye! _____

5. Planes do not fli in fog. _____

6. That is wy I cannot go. _____

Skill: Children will use a code to write spelling words. They will circle misspelled spelling words and will write them correctly.

Home Activity: Give your child a practice spelling test. Say each spelling word aloud, and use it in a sentence. Have your child write each spelling word.

Name _____

Special Words for Writing

little   who   year

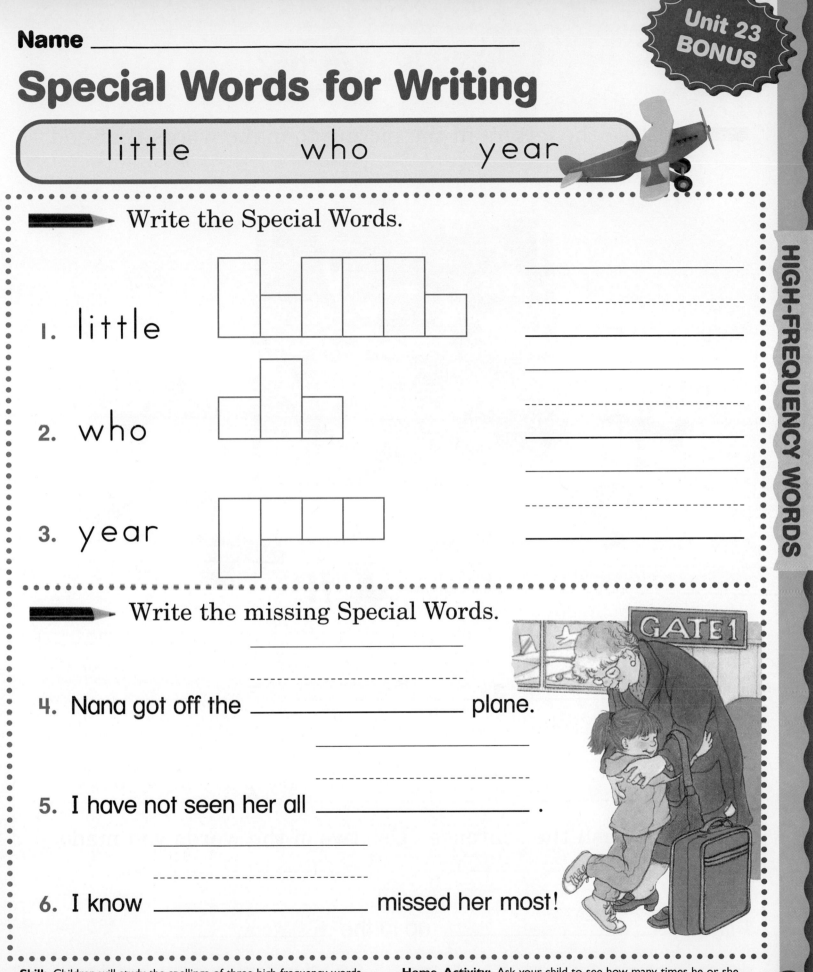

✏️ Write the Special Words.

1. little

2. who

3. year

HIGH-FREQUENCY WORDS

✏️ Write the missing Special Words.

_____

4. Nana got off the _____ plane.

_____

5. I have not seen her all _____ .

_____

6. I know _____ missed her most!

Skill: Children will study the spellings of three high-frequency words. They will write each word in configuration boxes, in isolation, and in a sentence.

Home Activity: Ask your child to see how many times he or she can find the three Special Words on a printed page from a book or a magazine.

Rhyming Words

PHONICS AND SPELLING

Use the letters in the picture to make words that end with **y**.

y

sh

j

f

sk

x

m

fl

dr

wh

1. _____

2. _____

3. _____

4. _____

5. _____

6. _____

Finish the sentence. Use two of the words you made.

I like to _____ up in the _____ .

Skill: Children will build new words by adding **y** to word parts. They will complete a sentence using two of the words they made.

Home Activity: Discuss the picture with your child. Share something you know about airports, or together, read a book about this topic.

Name _____

24 Review: Units 22–23

Unit 22   Words Spelled with th or wh (pages 169–174)

> this   that   white
> when   with   bath

Write the word that rhymes with each picture name.

1. _____

2. _____

Write the missing words.
Color the picture.

3. Taking a _____ is fun.

4. I am taking one _____ morning.

5. I take my fish in _____ me.

6. I get out _____ I am clean!

Skill: Children will write spelling words that rhyme with picture names. They will write spelling words to complete sentences.

Home Activity: Print each spelling word on a piece of heavy paper. Cut each word into four or five puzzle pieces. Have your child put the pieces together to make the spelling words.

24 Review

 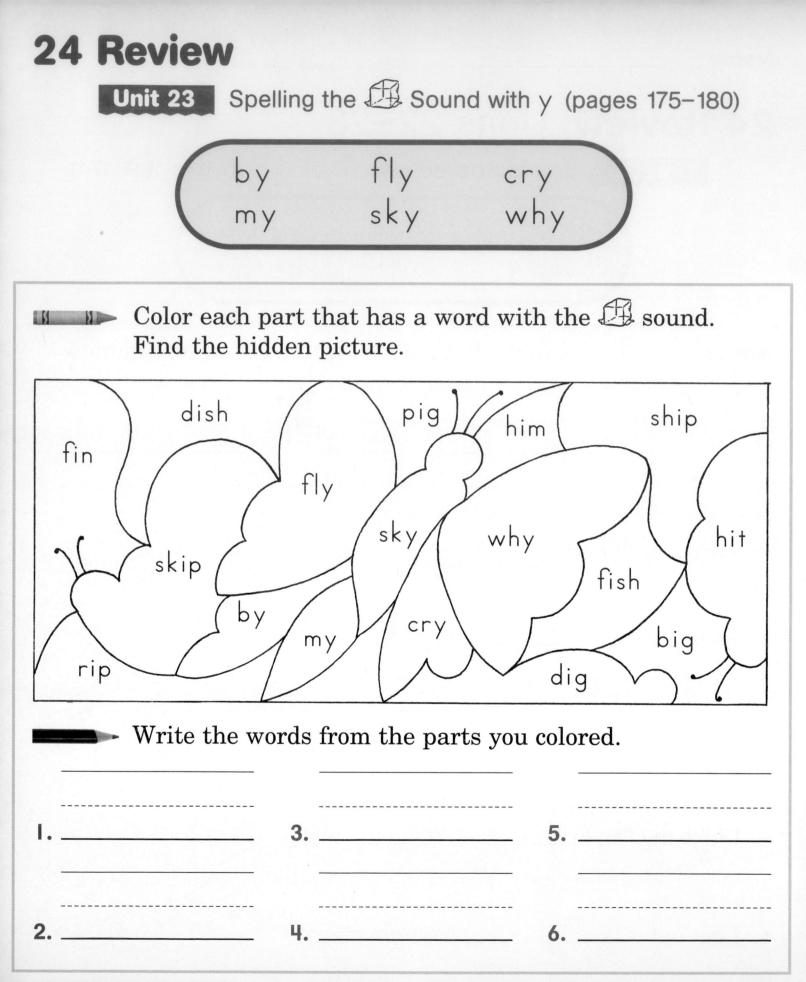

> by   fly   cry
> my   sky   why

Color each part that has a word with the sound. Find the hidden picture.

dish   pig   him   ship

fin   fly

sky   why   hit

skip   fish

by   cry   big

my

rip   dig

Write the words from the parts you colored.

1. _____

2. _____

3. _____

4. _____

5. _____

6. _____

Skill: Children will find a hidden picture by coloring shapes containing spelling words with the |ī| sound. They will write each spelling word.

Home Activity: Make dough by combining two cups of flour with one cup each of salt and water. Say each spelling word. Have your child use the dough to form the letters in each word.

The Man and His Caps
a folktale

Once there was a man who had caps for sale. He had the caps on his head.

First he had on his old brown cap. On top of the brown cap, he had orange caps. On top of the orange caps, he had blue caps. On top of the blue caps, he had yellow caps. And on the very top, he had red caps.

Every day the man would walk up one street and down another. He would call, "Caps for sale! Caps for sale!"

One day no one wanted a cap, not even a red one. "Well," thought the man, "I may as well get some sleep." So he walked off and found a big tree to sleep under. He made sure all his caps were in place, then he went to sleep.

When the man got up, he put up his hand to see if his caps were all in place. All he had was his old brown cap!

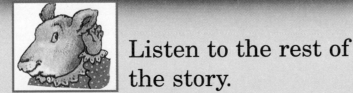

Listen to the rest of the story.

LITERATURE AND WRITING: A Story

Skill: Children will listen to and discuss a fictional story.

Home Activity: Have your child tell you about the story **The Man and His Caps.**

LITERATURE AND WRITING: A Story

1. Get Ready

Draw a picture of a funny hat.

2. Write

Write a story about the hat and the person who wears it. Use another sheet of paper.

Word Bank

it   top   like   with   ★very   ★who

3. Write More

4. Proofread

5. Make a Final Copy

Skill: Children will complete a prewriting activity in which they explore a topic by drawing. They will write a first draft, revise, proofread, and publish a fictional story.

Home Activity: Have your child read aloud his or her story. Together, talk about the story and the picture that goes with it.

Student's Handbook

Punchouts

Kangaroo Pocket Card
Lower- and Uppercase Letter Cards
Writer's Dictionary Covers and Word Bank
Word Strips for Units 1, 2, 4, and 5
Word Strips for Units 7, 8, 10, and 11
Word Strips for Units 13, 14, 16, and 17
Word Strips for Units 19, 20, 22, and 23

Name _____

Writing the Alphabet

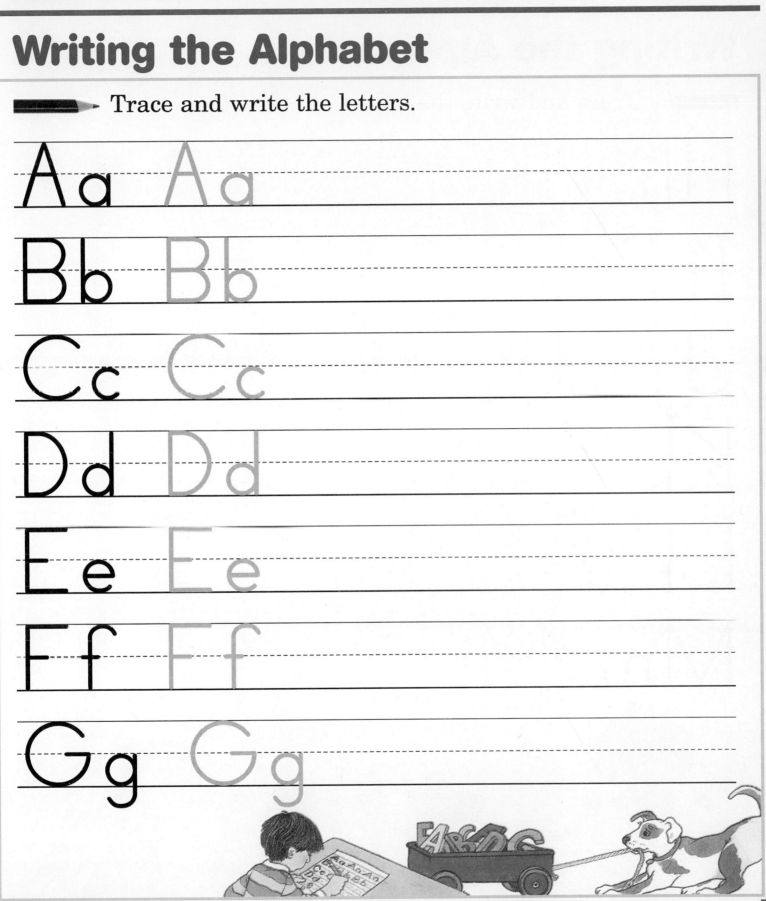

Trace and write the letters.

A a   A a

B b   B b

C c   C c

D d   D d

E e   E e

F f   F f

G g   G g

Skill: Children will trace and write upper- and lowercase forms of the letters **a** through **g**.

Name _____

Writing the Alphabet (continued)

Trace and write the letters.

Hh   Hh

Ii   Ii

Jj   Jj

Kk   Kk

Ll   Ll

Mm   Mm

Skill: Children will trace and write upper- and lowercase forms of
the letters **h** through **m**.

188

Writing the Alphabet (continued)

Trace and write the letters.

Nn Nn

Oo Oo

Pp Pp

Qq Qq

Rr Rr

Ss Ss

Skill: Children will trace and write upper- and lowercase forms of the letters **n** through **s**.

Writing the Alphabet (continued)

Trace and write the letters.

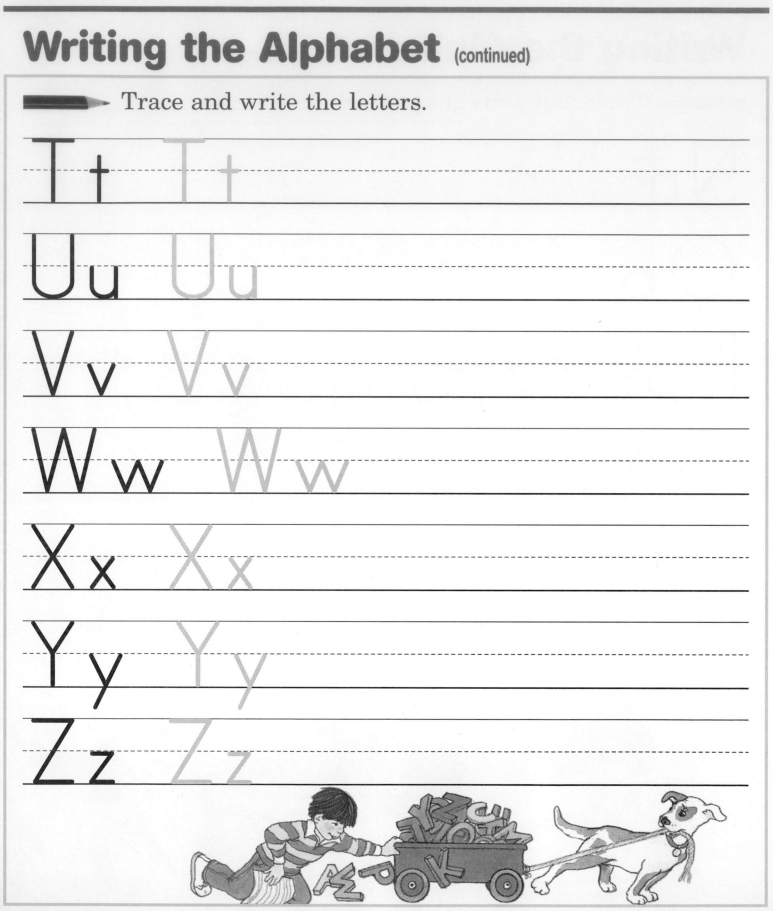

Tt Tt

Uu Uu

Vv Vv

Ww Ww

Xx Xx

Yy Yy

Zz Zz

Skill: Children will trace and write upper- and lowercase forms of the letters **t** through **z**.

Writer's Dictionary

The Alphabet

Beginning

Middle

End

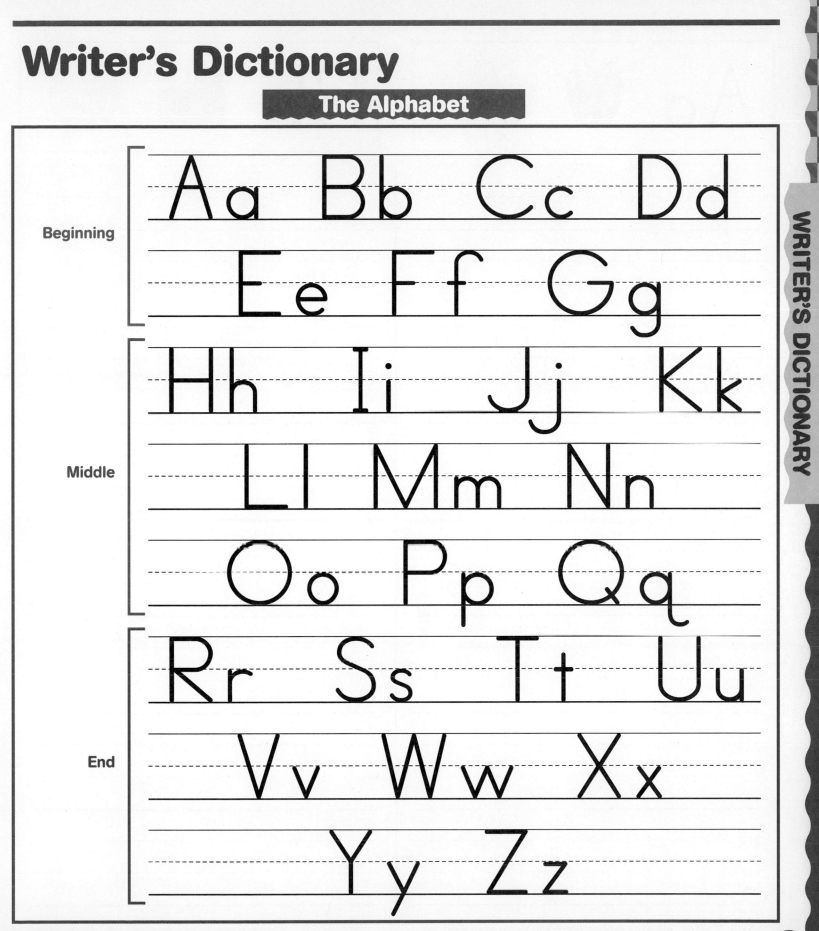

A a B b C c D d
E e F f G g
H h I i J j K k
L l M m N n
O o P p Q q
R r S s T t U u
V v W w X x
Y y Z z

WRITER'S DICTIONARY

Skill: Children will review the order of the letters in the alphabet and discuss the three parts of a dictionary.

A a

B b

Skill: Children will write spelling words and words from their own writing that begin with the letters **a** and **b**.

b

Cc

Skill: Children will write spelling words and words from their own writing that begin with the letters **b** and **c**.

c

Dd

Skill: Children will write spelling words and words from their own writing that begin with the letters **c** and **d**.

E e

F f

Skill: Children will write spelling words and words from their own writing that begin with the letters **e** and **f**.

f

G g

Skill: Children will write spelling words and words from their own writing that begin with the letters **f** and **g**.

Hh

Ii

Skill: Children will write spelling words and words from their own writing that begin with the letters **h** and **i**.

J j

K k

Skill: Children will write spelling words and words from their own writing that begin with the letters **j** and **k**.

L l

M m

Skill: Children will write spelling words and words from their own writing that begin with the letters **l** and **m**.

m

Nn

Skill: Children will write spelling words and words from their own writing that begin with the letters **m** and **n**.

O o

P p

Skill: Children will write spelling words and words from their own writing that begin with the letters **o** and **p**.

Qq

Rr

Skill: Children will write spelling words and words from their own writing that begin with the letters **q** and **r**.

Ss

S

Skill: Children will write spelling words and words from their own writing that begin with the letter **s**.

T t

t

Skill: Children will write spelling words and words from their own writing that begin with the letter **t**.

U u

V v

Skill: Children will write spelling words and words from their own writing that begin with the letters **u** and **v**.

W w | X x | Y y | Z z

Skill: Children will write spelling words and words from their own
writing that begin with the letters **w** through **z**.

Name _____

My Special Day

Word Bank

| red | yellow | purple | brown |
| black | blue | orange | green |

1 = 3 = 5 = 7 =

2 = 4 = 6 = 8 =

Instructions: Children will color, cut, and paste to make a paper birthday cake. They will write about a birthday celebration.

Materials: crayons, scissors, glue or paste, colored paper, pencils, and writing paper

Columbus Day

October

Word Bank

trip	sail	discover	Spain
America	Columbus	ocean	explore

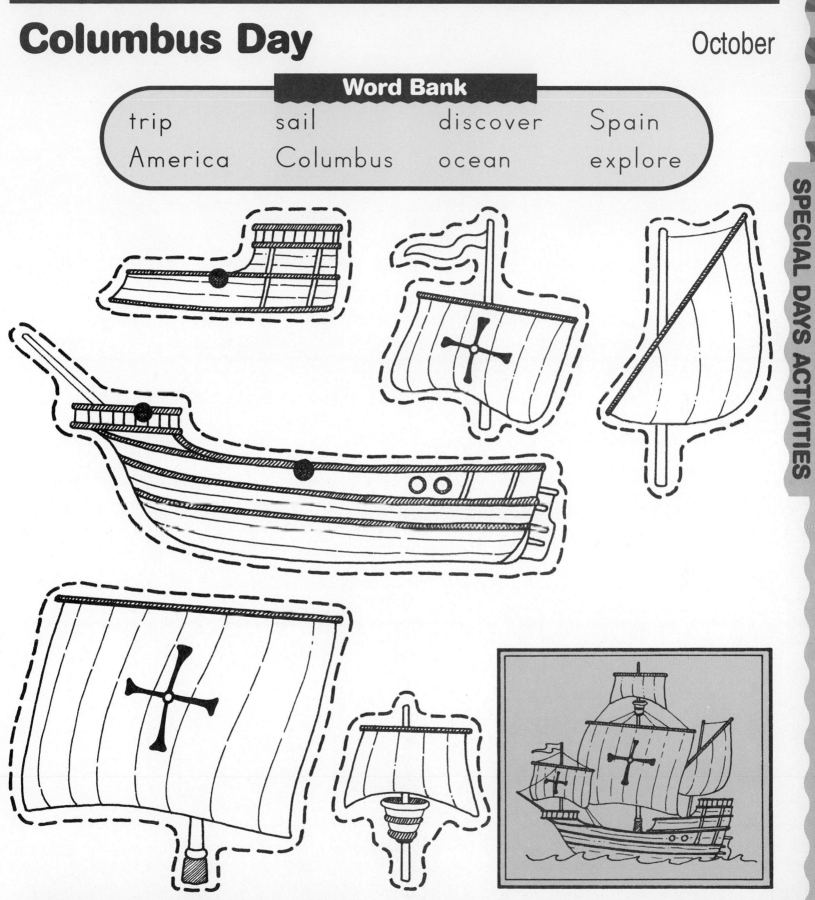

SPECIAL DAYS ACTIVITIES

Instructions: Children will color, cut, assemble, and paste puzzle pieces to make a paper ship. They will write about Christopher Columbus and his voyage to America.

Materials: crayons, scissors, glue or paste, colored paper, pencils, and writing paper

Name _____

Thanksgiving Day

November

Word Bank

Pilgrims   Native Americans   thanks   share

dinner   Mayflower   house   food

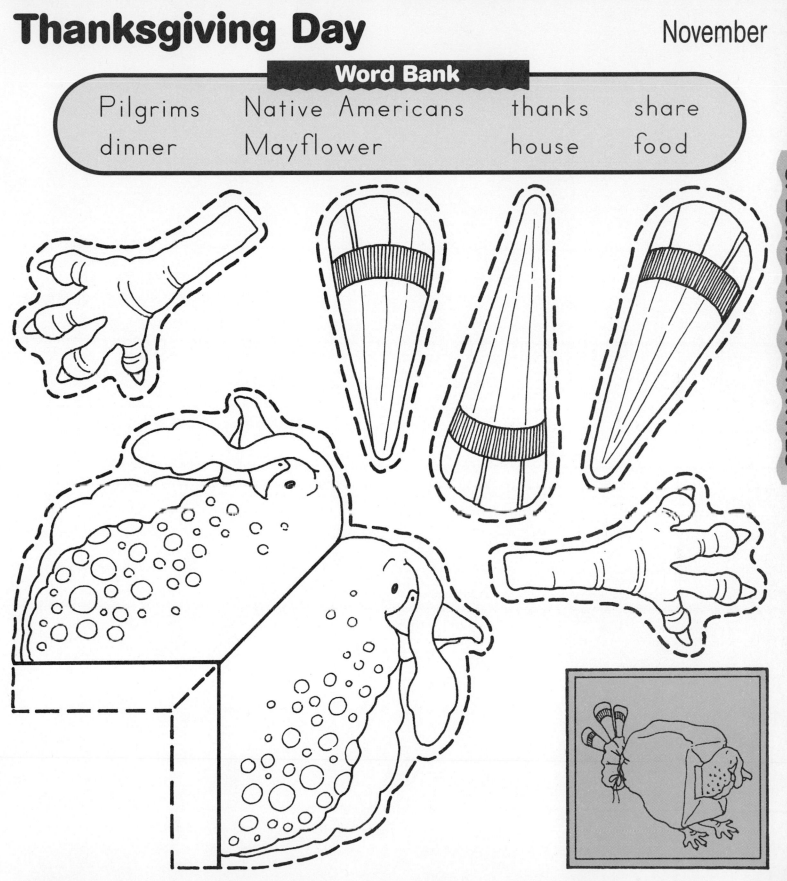

Instructions: Children will color, cut, fold, and paste to make a stuffed paper turkey. They will write about a Thanksgiving celebration.

Materials: brown paper lunch bags, used newspaper, string, crayons, scissors, tagboard, glue or paste, pencils, and writing paper

Name _____

International Arbor Day

December

Word Bank

tree   plant   woods   important   grow   leaf

Instructions: Children will color and cut to make four paper leaves. They will write about trees and why we need them.

Materials: crayons, scissors, pencils, and writing paper

Name _____

Martin Luther King, Jr. Day

January

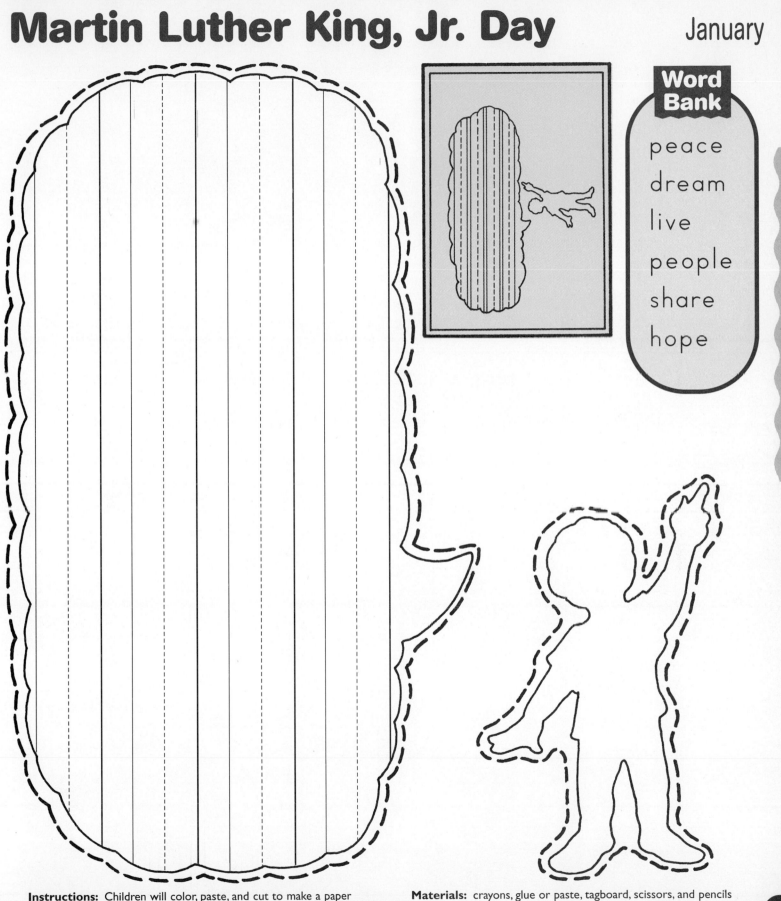

Word Bank

peace
dream
live
people
share
hope

Instructions: Children will color, paste, and cut to make a paper figure and a thought balloon. They will write about a dream for making the world a better place.

Materials: crayons, glue or paste, tagboard, scissors, and pencils

Valentine's Day

Word Bank

valentine
Dear
Mom
mine
Dad
love

Instructions: Children will fold, cut, and color to make a valentine. They will write a valentine message on the card.

Materials: scissors, crayons, and pencils

Name _____

Earth Day

March or April

Word Bank

earth	help	save	water
clean	litter	safe	air

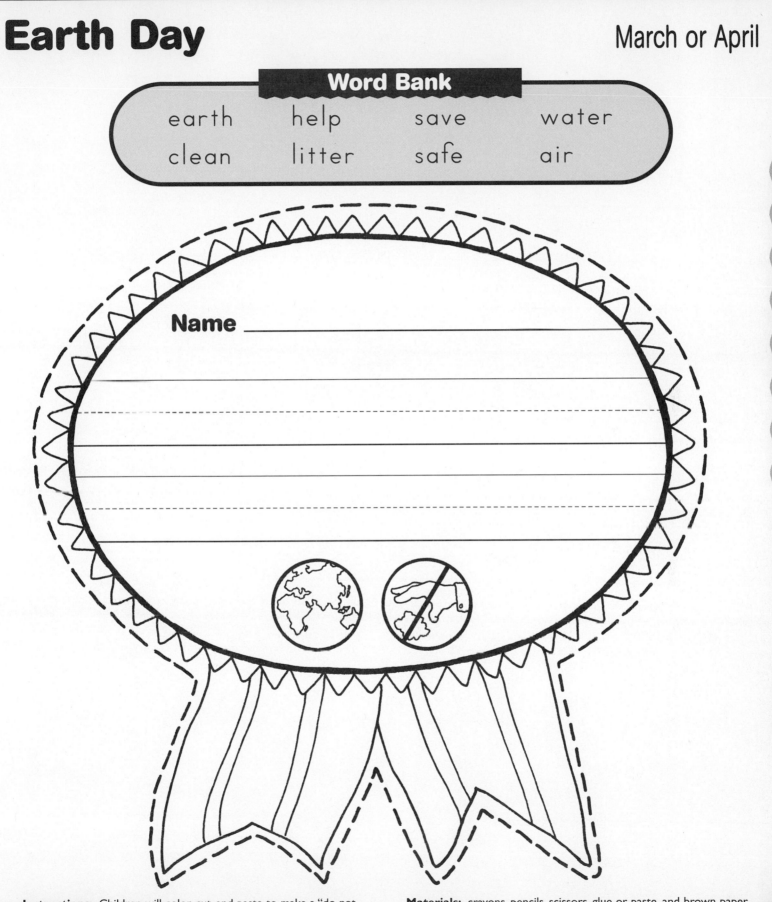

Name _____

Instructions: Children will color, cut, and paste to make a "do not litter" badge and bag. They will write a "do not litter" slogan on the badge.

Materials: crayons, pencils, scissors, glue or paste, and brown paper grocery bags

219

Name _____

International Children's Book Day April

Word Bank

story   book   read   favorite   title   author

Name _____

1. _____
2. _____
3. _____
4. _____
5. _____
6. _____

SPECIAL DAYS ACTIVITIES

Instructions: Children will cut, fold, and paste to make a bookmark for recording books they have read. They will write about one of the books.

Materials: scissors, glue or paste, crayons, and pencils

Children's Day

May

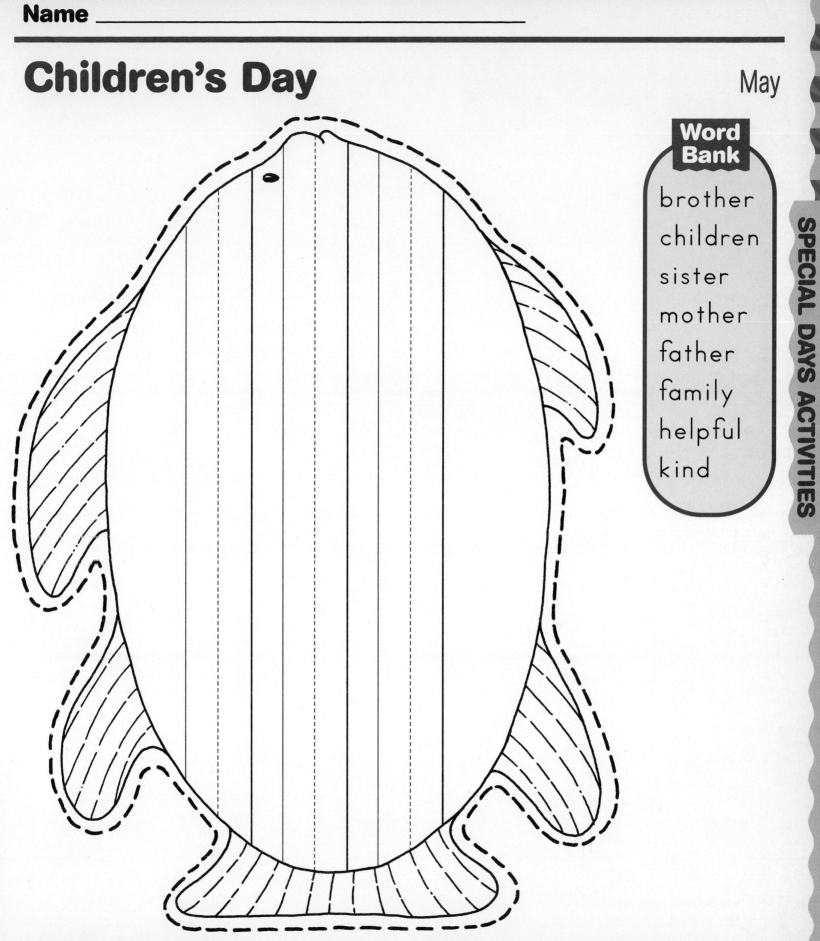

brother
children
sister
mother
father
family
helpful
kind

SPECIAL DAYS ACTIVITIES

Instructions: Children will color, paste, and cut to make a paper carp. They will write about themselves and their families.

Materials: crayons, glue or paste, tagboard, scissors, colored paper, and pencils